The Chancel, Stratford-On-Avon Church

THE OLD PARISH CHURCHES
OF WARWICKSHIRE
Mike Salter

CONTENTS

A GLOSSARY OF TERMS	Page	2
INTRODUCTION	Page	3
GAZETTEER	Page	15
FURTHER READING	Page	72
MAP	Back Cover	

Aston Cantlow Church

A GLOSSARY OF TERMS

Abacus   - A flat slab on top of a capital.

Apse   - Semi-circular or polygonal east end of a church containing an altar.

Ashlar   - Masonry of blocks with even faces and square edges.

Baldacchino   - A canopy supported on columns.

Ballflower   - Globular flower of three petals enclosing a ball. Current c1310-40.

Baroque   - A whimsical and odd form of the Classical architectural style.

Beakhead   - Decorative motif of bird or beast heads, often biting a roll-moulding.

Chancel   - The eastern part of a church used by the clergy.

Chevron Ornament - A Norman ornament with a continuous series of Vs forming a zig-zag.

Clerestory   - An upper storey of part of a church, pierced by windows.

Collar-Beam   - A tie-beam used higher up nearer the apex of a roof.

Corbel Table   - A row of corbels supporting the eaves of a roof.

Crossing Tower   - A tower built on four arches in the middle of a cruciform church.

Cruciform Church - A cross-shaped church with transepts forming the arms of the cross.

Cusp   - A projecting point between the foils in a foiled Gothic arch.

Dado   - The decorative covering of the lower part of a wall or screen.

Decorated   - A division of English Gothic architecture roughly from 1290 to 1360.

Dog Tooth   - Four cornered stars placed diagonally and raised pyramidally.

Early English   - The first division of English Gothic architecture from 1200 to 1290.

Easter Sepulchre - A recess in a chancel which received an effigy of Christ at Easter.

Elizabethan   - Of the time of Queen Elizabeth I (1558-1603).

Fan Vault   - A vault with blank fan-like tracery emanating from pendants.

Foil   - A lobe formed by the cusping of a circle or arch.

Four Centered Arch- A flat arch with each curve drawn from two compass points.

Hammerbeam Roof - A roof carried on arched braces set on beams projecting from a wall.

Herringbone Masonry - Courses of stones alternately sloping at 45 degrees to horizontal.

Hoodmould   - A projecting moulding above an arch or lintel to throw off water.

Indent   - A shape chiselled out of a stone to receive a memorial brass, etc.

Jacobean   - Of the time of King James I (1603-25).

Jamb   - The side of a doorway, window, or other opening.

King-Post   - An upright timber connecting a tie-beam with a collar-beam.

Lancet   - A long, comparatively narrow window, usually with a pointed head.

Light   - A compartment of a window.

Lintel   - A horizontal stone or beam spanning an opening.

Low-side Window - A window with a low sill allowing those outside a chancel to see in.

Lucarne   - A small opening in a spire to let light in.

Miserichord   - Bracket underneath hinged choir stall seat to support standing person.

Mullion   - A vertical member dividing the lights of a window.

Nave   - The part of a church in which the congregation sits.

Nook Shafts   - Shafts set in the angle of a pier, respond, or jamb of an opening.

Norman   - A division of English Romanesque architecture from 1066 to 1200.

Ogival Arch   - Arch of oriental origin with both convex and concave curves.

Perpendicular   - A division of English Gothic architecture from c1360 to 1540.

Pilaster   - Flat buttress or pier attatched to a wall. Used in Norman period.

Piscina   - A stone basin used for rinsing out holy vessels after a mass.

Plinth   - The projecting base of a wall.

Queen Posts   - Two vertical timbers connecting a tie-beam and a collar beam.

Quoins   - The dressed stones at the corners of a building.

Rere-Arch   - An arch on the inside face of a window embrasure or doorway.

Reredos   - A structure behind an altar. Usually sculpted or painted.

Respond   - A half-pier or column bonded into a wall, and carrying an arch.

Reticulation   - Tracery with a net-like appearence. Fashionable in c1330-60.

Rood Screen   - A screen with a crucifix mounted on it between a nave and chancel.

Saxon   - Division of the English Romanesque style from the 6th century to 1066.

Sedilia   - Seats for priests (usually three) on the south side of a chancel.

Spandrel   - The surface between two arches.

Tester   - A sounding board above a 17th century pulpit.

Tie-Beam   - A beam connecting the slopes of a roof at or near its foot.

Tracery   - The intersecting ribwork in the upper part of a later Gothic window.

Transom   - A horizontal member dividing the lights of a window.

Triforium   - A middle storey with an arcaded wall passage or blank arcading.

Triptych   - Three surfaces, usually sculpted or painted, joined by hinges.

Tuscan   - An order of Classical architecture.

Tympanum   - The space between the lintel of a doorway and the arch above it.

Venetian Window - Window with a square headed light set either side of an arched light.

Victorian   - Of the time of Queen Victoria (1837-1901).

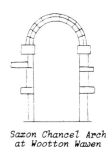

*Saxon Chancel Arch
at Wootton Wawen*

Beaudesert Church

INTRODUCTION

Warwickshire lies within what was the Saxon kingdom of Mercia in which Christianity was adopted after missionaries were sent from Northumbria in 653. By the time of the Norman conquest there were about 30 big parishes each with a mother church of stone and chapels-of-ease which were probably very humble buildings of wood. The only certain relics of these are parts of a lofty nave with a west gallery at Tredington and the lower parts of the central tower at Wootton Wawen which has narrow arches to north and south which led to small transeptal chapels called porticus, whilst there were wider arches to the nave to the west and chancel to the east, i.e. a cruciform plan. Both are only a couple of generations earlier than the invasion of 1066. Their openings, which are round headed, were small, and of the simplest possible form.

Little more has survived from the era of the first two generations of Norman rulers, just some herringbone masonry in the naves at Studley and Whitchurch (and possibly also Billesley), a sturdy chancel arch (now reset) at Wellesbourne, and a doorway at Ryton-on-Dunsmore, all c1100, and perhaps the crossing arches at Wolston with their evidence of tiny porticus on either side rather than fully developed transepts equal in width to the nave and chancel. William I laid much of Warwickshire waste after the rebellion of 1069 and it is unlikely that much work upon the ordinary parochial churches and chapels was undertaken until the 1130s.

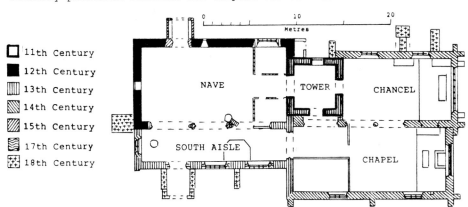

- ☐ 11th Century
- ■ 12th Century
- ▥ 13th Century
- ▨ 14th Century
- ▧ 15th Century
- ▩ 17th Century
- ⊞ 18th Century

PLAN OF WOOTTON WAWEN CHURCH

*Norman
Doorways
at Beaudesert
and Tredington*

In fact most of what we now call Norman in the county was built in the period 1160-1200, by the end of which a more intensive system of about 200 parishes had been laid out. Although most of the churches were rebuilt and remodelled over the succeeding centuries the actual number of churches and chapels did not significantly increase again until the late 18th century industrial revolution and the growth of suburbs led to the establishment of a whole series of new churches which lie outside the scope of this book which only considers work up to the 1760s.

Nearly a third of the 220 churches described in this book have some structural remains of the period 1160-1200. In several cases only some walling has survived later alterations, or a doorway or two, a single small round headed window, or maybe a font. Most 12th century churches as first built comprised a rectangular nave with the main entrance on the south side and perhaps a second doorway on the north, with a round arch in the east wall opening into an almost square chancel often only just large enough to contain the altar and attendant clergy. No examples in Warwickshire remain as complete and unaltered as the chapel at Heath in Shropshire but at Ansley, Ashow, Curdworth, Offchurch, Oxhill, and Wyken enough remains of both nave and chancel to get a feel of the appearence of such churches whilst Dosthill (transferred to Staffordshire in 1974) has a fairly unaltered small nave now sadly lacking its chancel. Indeed chancels are marginally less likely to survive unaltered, having been originally much too small for the ritual requirements of later periods, but there is a splendid specimen of c1170 at Berkswell. It has a crypt below with another (polygonal) crypt below the east end of the nave and a second Norman crypt survives from the large church at Warwick which was served by a college of secular canons. At Stoneleigh and Beaudesert there are signs that the chancels were intended to be vaulted. Each of these also has remains of the nave with one impressive doorway.

As population grew so more space was required for the congregation. This was usually provided in the form of aisles with lean-to roofs and arcades of round arches set upon circular piers. About 10 churches have remains of a single aisle of the period 1160-1200 whilst the churches at Tredington, Warmington, and Welford-on-Avon all had north and south aisles by 1200. Usually the arcades of these have fared better than the aisle outer walls which have been battered by the weather and breached for larger later windows to admit more light. About a dozen churches are known to have possessed a tower also by 1200, usually built against the west wall of the nave, although that at Handsworth stood beside the south wall. St Mary's at Nuneaton was cruciform with a central tower, a usual form for a monastic church. The towers are mostly heightened and otherwise remodelled in later periods. Of note are those of the 1190s at Ettington and Ilmington with pilasters, characteristically Norman, set at the corners and in the middle of the sides.

4

West Doorway at Kineton *Doorway, Pillerton Hersey*

Norman doorways are quite often elaborate affairs with one or more orders of columns with motifs such as scallops on the capitals and often chevrons, billets, roundels, beakheads, and other ornaments on the arch. Of c1140-50 are a doorway with an unusual square frame at Kenilworth thought to have been transferred from the nearby abbey church, and the boldly carved tympanum at Halford depicting a seated angel. There are more modestly decorated tympani at Alveston and Salford Priors. That at Stoneleigh is of c1175-85, as are other doorways of note at Beaudesert and Northfield.

About a third of the churches have structural remains from the 13th century, and there are others where there are more minor relics like a single window inserted in older walling. The pointed arch now reigns supreme, having been introduced in the 1190s, although round arches may still occur as late as c1215. There are fine chancels at Northfield and Pillerton Hersey but much of the work takes the form of added aisles or arcades remaining from such which were later rebuilt or widened. Nearly 40 churches have such remains and a third of these have evidence of two 13th century aisles. Notable are Napton and Burton Dassett which also have transepts. Stratford church has a central tower and transepts but the aisles of this period have not survived, whilst Alderminster has transepts but no aisles. Coventry had two major churches with aisles, towers, chapels, and porches by 1300, and there was another at Aston, but very little now remains of any of these in their 13th century form. A notable structure, although much renewed, and not a parochial church until the 19th century, is the Templar chapel of c1280 at Temple Balsall which is a single huge chamber. Over two dozen towers were begun during this period although most were altered or finished off later. Diagonal buttresses begin to come into fashion near the near of the century.

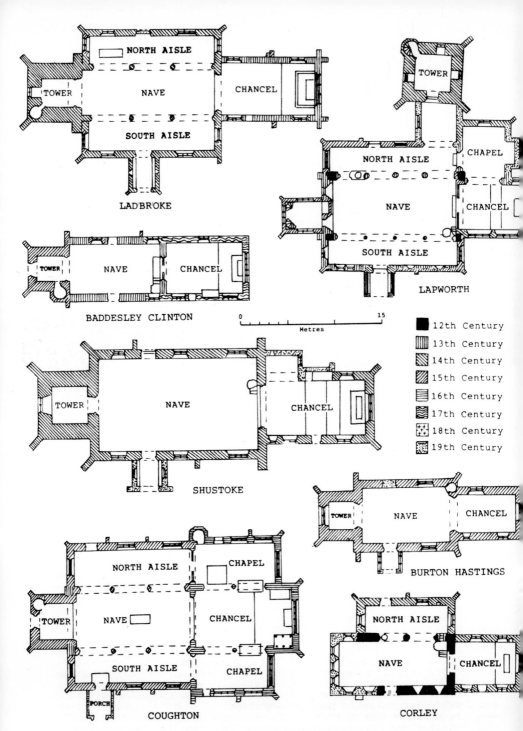

PLANS OF SEVEN MEDIEVAL WARWICKSHIRE CHURCHES

Tanworth Church   *Lapworth Church*

The central tower, transepts, and fine chancel with a north chapel raised over a vaulted sacristy at Solihull, and a number of churches with a fully aisled nave, west tower, and chancel all of about the same time as at Snitterfield and Hillmorton introduce us to the 14th century. The style now in vogue is known to historians as Decorated from a tendency for elaborate decoration of details such as window tracery, hoodmoulds, piers and capitals, etc, although the sort of exuberance found in some other counties does not manifest itself in Warwickshire. The ogival arch came into fashion c1320 and was commonly used over sedilia, piscinae, and the Easter Sepulchres then becoming popular. Arcade piers tend to be octagonal now instead of circular although quatrefoils and a few other variants occur occasionally as at Harborough Magna and King's Norton. Aisles added during this period (there are over thirty of them) tend to be wider and better lighted than before and sometimes also have porches. Thirty towers date from the 14th century, although a high proportion of spires upon them were not added until the 15th century. Most of the big churches of Tanworth and Tredington are of this period, and the smaller church at Shustoke. Of the 1340s specifically are the nave, originally a collegiate chancel, at Astley, and the single chamber at Maxstoke.

The Black Death of 1349 caused a lull in building activities until c1370. Then the huge and elaborate chancel at Warwick was begun, and the rebuilding of the two big churches at Coventry. By this time a new style, Perpendicular, was in fashion, initiated by work at Gloucester Abbey. The panelling found in some churches, especially that above the arcades reaching up to the clerestory at Holy Trinity, Coventry, shows clearly why the style is called thus. Clerestories themselves were now in fashion for parish churches although they existed on monastic and cathedral churches centuries earlier. Of a dozen towers likely to be of c1370-1400 those of the former friary churches at Atherstone and Christ-church, Coventry are of note, being octagonal over a narrow rectangular transept-less central space between nave and chancel. The much smaller turret over a triple arch at Baginton seems to be a copy of this idea.

Halford, 13th century

Quinton, 14th century

King's Norton, 15th century

Packwood, c1500

Warwick, c1700

FIVE WARWICKSHIRE CHURCH TOWERS

West Front, Baxterley

St Philip's
Cathedral,
Birmingham

The Perpendicular style remained in fashion right through the 15th century, and, though usually in a debased form, still occasionally is seen as late as the mid 17th century. Nearly sixty churches have towers of the period 1400-1540, and many others have bell stages and/or spires of this era, and inserted windows in older walls are almost universal. At Lapworth and Wootton Wawen the addition of clerestories and parapets to the naves along with other inserted windows, etc, give the churches a misleading aura of being entirely of this period. In fact complete or nearly complete 15th century churches are not common in Warwickshire. Those at knowle, Henley-in-Arden, and Weston-On-avon, plus the guild chapel at Stratford are the only ones, though Brinklow is also mostly of this period. Much of the two big churches at Coventry is, or was before restoration, 15th century, although begun c1370 and with extensions still being made in the 1540s. Stratford has a particularly fine chancel and more than a dozen churches have an aisle of this period, while others had older arcades or aisles replaced. For scale and quality, however, pride of prace goes to the sumptuous Beauchamp Chapel of the 1440s and 50s at Warwick where the walls are blank panelled inside and out. It has a fan vault instead of the usual low pitched roof with bosses for this period. A number of roofs remain from this period but few call for any special comment. Coughton is an interesting instance of an early 16th 16th century chancel with chapels on eith side being added to an aisled nave of the late 15th century.

At about the time of the Reformation of the Church by Henry VIII in the 1530s and 40s the building boom ceased in parish churches. There are chapels of the 1550s at Rowington and Sutton Coldfield and a few of the clerestories may be of the same period. Then there is a barren period to which little other than the odd window or so can be assigned until the major rebuilding of Astley church begun in 1607. A chancel at Wolvey is dated 1624, then there is another gap until the 1660s and 70s when chapels were added at Stoneleigh and Idlicote and the private chapel at Compton Wyniates was rebuilt after a Civil War damage, whilst a chancel was rebuilt at Leamington Hastings. In the 1680s a complete new church was erected at Honington, and of c1700 are the tower at Wishaw and an aisled nave and tower on a huge scale and in a debased Gothic style at Warwick. About a dozen churches are essentially 18th century buildings but most of them were altered in the 19th century. Preston-On-Stour, Over Whittacre and St Philip's at Birmingham preserve their original character, and the latter two are in the Classical style rather than Gothic. New churches of the 19th century do not concern us here but it should be noted that nearly all the churches suffered alterations and restoration then.

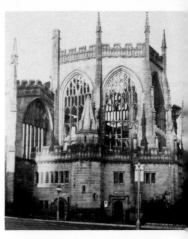

Knowle Church

The apse,
St Michael,
Coventry

Doorways and masonry styles can help to date different parts of old churches but usually the shape and style of the windows give the best evidence. Some caution should be exercised, however, as the windows may either be later insertions or earlier openings repositioned. During the 12th century windows gradually increased in size from small round headed openings of the Saxon and Early Norman periods. Most of the windows of this period are plain externally but there are east windows with shafts and hoodmoulds of c1170-80 at Berkswell and Beaudesert.

By 1200 the standard window type was the long lancet, usually with a pointed head. Early 13th century single lancets can be seen in the chancel at Yardley and the tower at Fillongley. By c1250-60 they began to be used in multiples. A pair remain at Chadshunt, and triples under segmental outer arches at Northfield. The east window at Pillerton Hersey goes one stage further in that above three lancets is a circle containing a cusped quatrefoil. This is what is known as plate tracery. The next development, c1280, is geometrical tracery where there are several such circles containing foiled shapes as at Temple Balsall and Brailes.

A very popular design evolved c1275 which remained in used until the 1340s is Y-tracery in which a single mullion branches at the top. Where there are three or more lights the same idea gives intersected tracery also very common, as at Rowington and Snitterfield. Sometimes there are cusped foils within the intersections as in the east window at Solihull of c1300. The chancel side windows there have a floral form typical of the Decorated style then in vogue. Sometimes the intersections themselves are left unadorned but the main lights have a trefoiled head. At Aston Cantlow there are separate trefoils above the trefoil headed main lights and below the branching arms of a Y. The more complex floral patterns found in some counties rarely appear in Warwickshire but slightly more adventurous designs of c1345 can be seen at Astley. A common design of c1320-50 is reticulation or net-like tracery using the new ogival arch.

Mullions rising directly to the main arch with or without subsidiary tracery are a hallmark of the Perpendicular style. Of c1570-80 are the chancel side windows at Atherstone and Mancetter with the central light having nothing other than five cusps at the top, whilst the side lights are formed into cinquefoiled cusped lancets by subsidiary arches. Knowle illustrates various designs current c1400. Some windows have a varient on the type described above but with the main light having a transom near the top with cusping below it. Other windows have an elongated type of reticulation and some have no tracery at all, just cusped heads to the lights. Square headed windows of two or more cusped headed lights, seen as early as c1330-40 at Leamington Hastings, are common in the 15th and 16th centuries. More ambitious 15th century windows can be seen at Warwick, Stratford, and in three of the churches at Coventry. Gradually arches get flatter and after 1500 cusping begins to disappear. Work of c1520 at Coughton contrasts starkly with late 15th century work there.

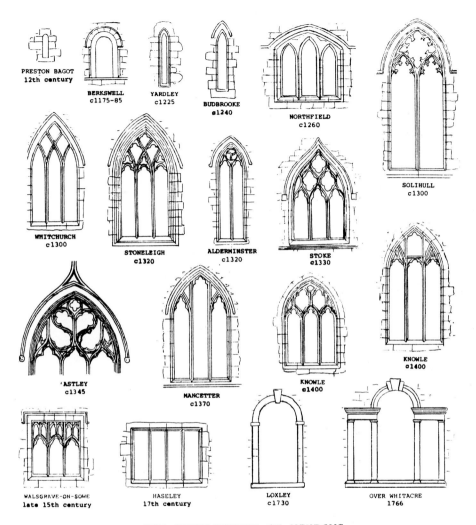

PRESTON BAGOT
12th century

BERKSWELL
c1175-85

YARDLEY
c1225

BUDBROOKE
c1240

NORTHFIELD
c1260

SOLIHULL
c1300

WHITCHURCH
c1300

STONELEIGH
c1320

ALDERMINSTER
c1320

STOKE
c1330

ASTLEY
c1345

MANCETTER
c1370

KNOWLE
c1400

KNOWLE
c1400

WALSGRAVE-ON-SOWE
late 15th century

HASELEY
17th century

LOXLEY
c1730

OVER WHITACRE
1766

THE DEVELOPMENT OF WINDOWS

Late 16th and 17th century windows are not common in Warwickshire churches. Usually they are simple rectangles with mullions and without tracery as at Haseley. Cross-windows with a transom added to the mullion occur at Barcheston, and occasionally the lights are arched, with or without cusps. Older forms were revived, as at Hillmorton where there is intersected tracery in a window of 1640. Only at Warwick c1700 do larger and more interesting windows occur. They are late medieval in overall character though to a very individual design. Alcester of c1730 and Preston-On-Stour of the 1750s were Gothic too. Of buildings in the classical style with large untraceried round arched windows only that of St Philip, now the cathedral, at Birmingham, remains unchanged. The Victorians experimented with all the older styles and examples of their period occur frequently in the churches as a result of restoration. Some of their windows reproduce what was there before, but others ignore the original form or are in any case completely new openings.

Sutton Coldfield Font

Bickenhill Font

Door at Caldecote

When first built the churches were generally dimly lit and sparsely furnished. Larger windows inserted later admitted more light if fitted with plain glass, but from the 14th century onwards they were provided with stained glass showing biblical scenes, lives of saints, or heraldry of benefactors. About 40 churches retain some old glass although a lot of it is fragmentary and has in some cases been transferred from other windows, or even from another church. More survives at the churches of Cherington, Coughton, Mancetter, and Merevale. Wall paintings used to be very common but are generally now faded or painted or plastered over.

Floors were originally of rammed earth covered once a year with new rushes and paving stones were only introduced much later. The altar step might be tiled and tiles as early as the 13th century, often ex situ, survive in a few churches. Early congregations stood during the services and only in the late medieval period were benches provided. They often have ends with tracery and poppy-heads. Late medieval choir stalls now only remain in a few churches. At Knowle and Astley the seats are the hinged type called miserichords with carved scenes underneath. Medieval pulpits rarely survive although there are stone examples at Rowington and Holy Trinity, Coventry. Long sermons only became fashionable in the 16th century, and 17th century pulpits are much more common. Several have classical motifs. Often a more modern pulpit will have older panels used in it. Two and three decker pulpits with sounding boards were sometimes installed from the 1670s onwards but few of them now remain. Communion rails of c1660-1760, on the other hand, are quite common. Medieval doors survive occasionally. Much more frequent is for the woodwork to be later but with splendid 12th or 13th century hinges. Plate and other valuables were kept in chests secured with strong locks which frequently survive.

From the 14th century onwards the custom arose of closing off the chancel with a screen. Some of these bore lofts which were used for the performance of plays which were of importance in conveying God's Word in the days when much of the services were sung or spoken in Latin and sermons in English were not yet fashionable. They were also used by the church musicians. Organs only came into general use in the 19th century, although the greater churches had them by the time of the Reformation. The lofts bore a crucifixion scene on them called a Rood and this caused most to be removed by the end of the 17th century. Later restorations swept away most of the rest. One loft however survives at Wormleighton. Screens survive more frequently, mostly from the 15th century, but at Long Itchington, Shotteswell, and Wolfhampcote they are as early as the 14th century. Screens closing off chapels and transetps remain in a few churches, and there are parclose screens in the nave at Wootton Wawen.

The item of furniture most likely to survive from medieval times is a font. Later medieval fonts tend to have simple motifs like quatrefoils or blank tracery but Norman fonts sometimes have bolder and more complex carvings. There are interesting examples with motifs sometimes seeming barbaric at Coleshill, Curdworth, Oxhill, and Sutton Coldfield.

Tomb of unknown 15th century knight at Wootton Wawen

There are about four dozen effigies, two dozen brasses, and 6 incised slabs inlaid with pitch earlier than 1540 in the old parish churches of Warwickshire. Studley has another type of monument, a late 13th century coffin lid with a fine floriated cross and a lombardic script inscription. The effigies begin with the early 13th century priest at Avon Dassett and the abbess at Polesworth. Next comes the late 13th century knight at Merevale. Several churches have a 14th century knight, lady, or priest. Hillmorton has one of each, the lady being of high quality, but best of all is the monument at Warwick to Thomas Beauchamp, d1369.

Warwick has the best 15th century effigy too with that of Richard Beauchamp, d1439. It is of bronze gilt with copper. All the other effigies are of stone or alabaster. Collections of effigies can be seen at Astley, Aston, and St Martin at Birmingham. Many of them are now very mutilated. Often tombs and effigies have been moved around by restorers and one tomb at Aston suffered the indignity of heating pipes being run round it in a most unsightly way.

The series of brasses begins with the fine knights and ladies of 1401-30 at Baginton, Warwick, Wixford, Quinton, and Merevale. There are three brasses at Coleshill starting with a priest of c1425. There is a judge of 1476 at Middleton, and male civilians begin c1500 at Hampton-in-Arden and Withybrook.

Brass at Warwick

13

Monuments of William Shakespeare and Judith Combe at Stratford-on-Avon

Over a hundred monuments of the period 1540-1700 are mentioned in the gazetteer, and a further forty of the 18th century. There are numerous inscriptions with little or no adornment which are not here mentioned. Effigies on tomb chests remained fashionable throughout Elizabeth I's reign and into the 17th century. Gradually, in the 1560s and 70s, tombs begin to display Rennaissance details along with the well established Gothic features. Aston has three effigies of this period and there are two separate monuments at each of Coleshill, Monks Kirby, Handsworth, Upper Shuckburgh, Coughton, Chesterton, Charlecote, Compton Wyniates and Middleton. One of the Handsworth monuments depicts a man in a shroud. The Earl of Leicester's tomb at Warwick of the 1590s has a flat arch over it carried on columns on the side away from the wall. At Ettington and Coughton the tombs have canopies carried on four and six posts. At Warwick is a six poster tomb without an effigy. Sometimes the figures are only semi-recumbent. A common layout as at Newbold-on-Avon, Clifford Chambers, etc, is for a man and wife to be portrayed kneeling facing each other across a prayer desk. Single kneeling figures are at Caldecote and Middleton. The poet William Shakespeare has a frontal half figure in the church at Stratford. This is a type often used for scholars and divines. There are two dozen brasses and five incised slabs of the period 1540-1640. Most are of rather poor quality and some, like that at Solihull, show a couple kneeling towards each other upon a fairly modestly sized rectangular plate. Only the earlier ones, like the judge at Aston, c1545, tend to have larger separately cut out figures.

The emphasis on effigies decreased during the 17th century and by the 18th century mural tablets with lengthy inscriptions became normal. Some of these are made of marble and other fine materials. They may have architectural surrounds with columns, pediments, urns, cherubs, symbols of death or a profession, heraldry, and other adornments. Some are very large and impressive monuments. Effigies as late as the 18th century do appear at Newbold-On-Avon, Ettington, and Yardley.

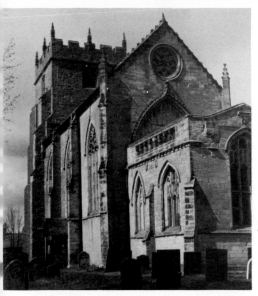

Astley
Church

Alcester
Church

GAZETTEER OF CHURCHES

ALCESTER *St Nicholas*   SP 091575

Of the medieval church there now remain only the late 13th century tower
with a 15th century top, and part of an ornate early 16th century screen.
The nave and aisles were built in 1729-30 by the Woodwards of Chipping
Campden and have a Gothic exterior and a classical interior with Tuscan
columns, a coved ceiling over the nave, and flat ceilings on the aisles.
The window tracery and the east end are of 1870-1. There are a splendid
brass chandelier of 1733 and several monuments of note, the earliest
being the recumbent effigies of Sir Fulke Greville, d1559, and his wife,
that with columns and a segmental pediment to John Brandis, d1724, and
the curious tablet with pyramids and putti to William Halford, d1731.

ALDERMINSTER *St Mary & Holy Cross*   SP 230486

The nave is Norman although the porch and most of the other features
except for the north doorway and one window are of 1884. Pershore Abbey
became patron in 1193 and immediately began to rebuild the church to a
cruciform plan. The crossing arches and north transept are of the 1190s,
whilst the south transept, tower, and chancel are about a generation
later. The chancel and nave each have one 14th century window. There was
formerly a chapel, probably of Our Lady, east of the north transept.
A font of the 1660s now lies in the porch.

ALLESLEY *All Saints*   SP 302806

The two round arched western bays of the south arcade are Norman. The
eastern bay, the widened aisle itself, the south porch, and the chancel
are in their present form of 1863. The tower and the three bay north
arcade are 13th century. The north aisle and chapel, and the spire with
three sets of lucarnes alternating in different directions are of the
14th century. The earliest of several tablets are late 17th century.

ALVESTON *St James*   SP 233564

When a new church was built in 1839 only the 18th century brick chancel
of the old church further north was left standing. It contains a Norman
tympanum with flowers and two animals, a 17th century pulpit, and the
rustic effigy of Nicholas Lane, d1595, probably intended to be upright.

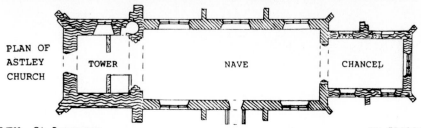

PLAN OF
ASTLEY
CHURCH

TOWER | NAVE | CHANCEL

ANSLEY *St Laurence* SP 290926

The nave and chancel both have Norman masonry and pilaster buttresses.
There are two original doorways, one reset in the three bay north aisle
of 1913, and a chancel arch with volutes and leaves on the capitals and
on one abacus two monsters swallowing a man. The chancel was re-windowed
in the 14th century, and in the 18th was doubled in length and given a
reredos with black Tuscan columns and a communion rail. The altarpiece
is probably 17th century Dutch work. The fine diagonally buttressed west
tower with transomed bell openings, and the clerestory and two southern
windows are 15th century. There are box pews, fragments of medieval glass
in a north window, and pedestals of 1700 and 1727 formerly for urns.

ANSTY *St James* SP 400836

The chancel is late 13th century. The nave south side and north arcade
are 15th century. The tower was added in 1856.

ARLEY *St Wilfrid* SP 284906

In a restored recess is an effigy of a priest of c1350 with angels at
his pillow. The chancel, with fragments of original glass in one north
window, was rebuilt in his time, as was the nave, and a west tower was
added. However, the nave retains a Norman clasping pilaster buttress at
the NW corner, and the south side except for the doorway is Victorian.

ARROW *St James* SP 083565

The church was heavily restored in 1865 when the north aisle and chapel
were built. The chancel and the tomb recesses in the north aisle wall
are 14th century. The nave has renewed 13th century windows and a much
repaired Norman doorway. The west tower dates from 1767. The pulpit
is of c1640, and there is a Crucifixion from the head of a former cross.

ASHOW *Assumption* SP 313703

The nave and chancel are both Norman, with a doorway and two windows on
the north. The whitewashed arcading in the chancel may be original. East
of the main doorway is a blocked 13th century one. The nave south wall
was rebuilt c1800 and the roof with tie-beams, kingposts and queenposts
is perhaps 16th century. The west tower is 15th century. There are box
pews, an 18th century pulpit, and parts of a Flemish triptych of c1550.

ASTLEY *St Mary* SP 312894

The present nave was originally the spacious three bay chancel of Sir
Thomas Astley's fine collegiate church of the 1340s which was allowed
to decay from the 1540s until the tower fell in c1600. It has splendid
three light windows with flowing tracery. Roughly contemporary with the
choir stalls of c1400 with Apostles and Prophets painted on their backs
is the seven light east window. When Richard Chamberlaine remodelled the
building in c1607-10 for use as a parish church a new chancel was added
and the lower part of the original east window was removed and the rest
blocked up. He also added the very large and massive west tower. Both
parts look late medieval outside, but the chancel was given a plaster
ceiling in c1800. There is a brass to a lady of c1400 and now arranged
together are alabaster figures of Sir Edward Grey, Lord Ferrers, d1457,
and the wives of Edward Grey, Lord Lisle, and Thomas Grey, Marquess of
Dorset. There are a few fragments of medieval glass, the pulpit and the
lectern are splendid pieces of c1680 and there is Flemish triptych.

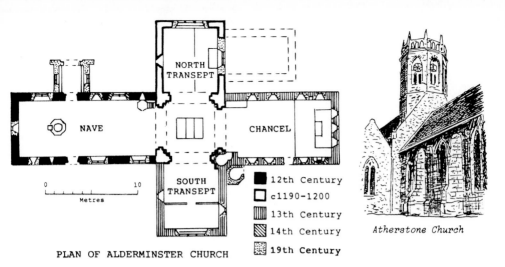

12th Century
c1190-1200
13th Century
14th Century
19th Century

PLAN OF ALDERMINSTER CHURCH

Atherstone Church

ASTON *St Peter & St Paul*   SP 083899

Aston Church is mentioned in the Domesday Book of 1086. The parish was large and eventually had six medieval chapels-of-ease. The present huge church at Aston is mostly of 1879-90 and 1908. The medieval church was the same width as the present building but was shorter. From it survive the large 15th century west tower with a lofty spire partly rebuilt in 1776-7, some parts of a 14th century cross, and many monuments. There are also four 15th century stalls from St Margaret's Church at Leicester.

The monuments have been reset and some are rather battered. Upon a tomb chest in the chancel are effigies of a knight of c1360 and a lady of c1469 which were probably removed to Aston from Maxstoke Priory at the Dissolution. There are also a damaged effigy of a 15th century knight and an elaborate monument to Sir Thomas Erdington, d1453, and his wife Joan or Anne Harcourt, d1417. The monument was probably made after their son built and endowed a chantry chapel at Aston in 1459. The Erdington Chapel contains a similar effigy, probably Sir William Harcourt, plus effigies of William Holte, d1514, and his wife Joan, an alabaster wall monument with kneeling figures of Edward Holte, d1592, and Dorothy, his wife, d1627, a mural monument with weeping putti to Sir Thomas Holte, (builder of Aston Hall), and memorials to Sir Charles Holte, d1722, Sir Lister Holte, d1770, and another Sir Charles Holte, d1782. Under the tower are the brasses of Thomas Holte, Justice of North Wales, Lord of Aston, d1545, and his wife Margaret, and in the south aisle are tablets to Sir John Bridgman, d1710, Edward Brandwood, d1731, and others.

ASTON CANTLOW *St John The Baptist*   SP 136600

The 13th century west tower has a 15th century top. The north aisle with a west turret is 14th century. The chancel of c1290-1300 has sedilia and piscina and fine windows. The font with flowers in quatrefoils and bearded men is 15th century. The pulpit is Jacobean, and the reredos has traceried panels probably from a screen. There are six bench ends with poppy heads. One window has fragments of old glass. A sculptured scene of the Nativity can be seen on the outside of the north wall.

ATHERSTONE *St Mary*   SP 308979

The spacious chancel with a five light east window and three light side windows, plus the octagonal tower raised over a square crossing date from about the time an independant chapel was taken over by Austin Friars in the 1370s. The large nave and aisles are entirely of 1849. The font with symbols of the Evangelists and Instruments of The Passion is medieval.

17

Baginton Church

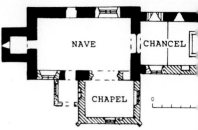

PLAN OF BARTON-ON-THE-HEATH CHURCH

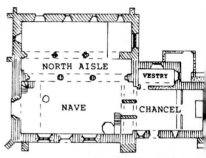

PLAN OF BAGINTON CHURCH

AUSTREY *St Nicholas*   SK 296063

The west tower is late 13th century. The church to which it was added
was replaced by a new aisled nave of four bays with lofty arches and a
chancel in the early 14th century. The latter was refaced and given new
windows in 1844-5. One aisle window has fragments of old glass. There
is a monument of c1705 to three sons of Thomas Monck.

AVON DASSETT *St John The Baptist*   SP 410499

The church was entirely rebuilt in 1868 but contains an effigy of c1210
of a Deacon holding a scroll on a low chest with three short colonettes.

BADDESLEY CLINTON *St Michael*   SP 203714

A later inscription in the tower records that it was erected by Nicholas
Brome in Henry VII's reign. The nave has windows of about the same era
but earlier masonry. A second inscription records the rebuilding of the
chancel in 1634, and the same year appears on the screen. The restored
east window glass is early 16th century. The tomb chest of Sir Edward
Ferrers, d1564, and his wife is still entirely gothic in its design.

BAGINTON *St John The Baptist*   SP 343747

The octagonal bell turret of c1380 set over three arches of equal width
between the nave and chancel is a great rarity. The chancel has several
features of the 13th century and with it go the nave masonry and north
arcade of three bays. Instead of being widened as usual the narrow aisle
was in the 14th century given a wide outer aisle with its own arcade
of quatrefoil shaped piers. The outer aisle has a tomb recess and some
fragments of old glass in one window. The pulpit, box pews, and west
gallery are late 18th century, but the communion rail and panelling are
of the 1720s, whilst the screen of the Bromley family vault is of 1677.
There are fine brasses of Sir William Bagot, d1407, builder of the castle
and his wife Margaret, the indent of another brass in the outer aisle,
a monument with figures of Faith, Hope, and Charity to Mrs Campion, d1632
and a tablet to Mrs Bromley, d1742.

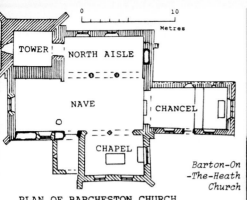

Barton-On
-The-Heath
Church

PLAN OF BARCHESTON CHURCH

BARCHESTON *St Martin*   SP 266399

The three bay north arcade looks Late Norman although one pier is dated
1631. The cross windows in the aisle would go with that date. The tower
walls towards the aisle and nave seem late 13th century but the outer
walls are late 14th century. The priest had chambers on the upper levels.
The chancel and south doorway are early 13th century. Several windows
are 14th century, like the south chapel with a two bay arcade, and the
porch which adjoins it. Tho font has cusped panels, and tracery panels
on the stem. There are an incised slab to a civilian of c1500, a brass
to the priest Hugh Humphray, d1530, and effigies on a tomb chest in the
chapel of William Willington, d1555, and his wife.

BARFORD *St Peter*   SP 273609

The church was rebuilt in 1844 leaving only the 15th century west tower
and several monuments of which the earliest are a defaced 14th century
female effigy and a tablet to Thomas Dugard, d1683.

BARSTON *St Swithin*   SP 207780

This is a small church consisting of a west tower, nave, and chancel,
built of brick with stone quoins in 1721, but remodelled in 1899. The
only notable original fitting is the twisted baluster communion rail.

BARTON-ON-THE-HEATH *St Laurence*   SP 256325

The nave doorways and chancel arch on half round responds with trumpet
scalloped capitals are Late Norman. The tower and one chancel northern
window are also earlier than 1200. The south chapel with reticulated
window tracery, the east window with ball flower ornament, and the tower
top with a saddleback roof are 14th century. The nave north window and
font with flowers in quatrefoils are 15th century. There is 14th and
15th century glass in the north windows. On the chancel floor is a brass
to Edmund Bury, d1559.

BAXTERLEY *Dedication Unknown*   SP 256970

The small chancel of c1200 has two tiny original windows and a priest's
doorway on the north side, an unusual location. In the 14th century a
narrow south aisle with a tomb recess was added. The arcade was later
done away with, perhaps in the 17th century, the date of the present
west front with a tiny tower projecting within the nave. In the 1870s
the south side was refaced and a north aisle, porch, and vestry added.

BEARLEY *St Mary*   SP 183605

The features are mostly of the rebuilding of 1961-2 when a blocked up
Norman north doorway was reopened, but the masonry is mostly medieval.

*Berkswell
Church*

BEAUDESERT *St Nicholas*   SP 153661

The two bay chancel with clasping pilaster buttresses and a fine east
window and chancel arch with two orders of columns, and the nave south
wall with one original window and a splendid south doorway with multiple
chevrons and three orders of columns are Late Norman. The chancel has
unusually thick walling and was intended to be vaulted although such was
not provided until 1865. The nave was shortened when a tower was built
in place of the south half of its west end in the 15th century, and then
or later a new nave north wall was built within the original wall line.
There are 15th century bench ends and two bells of c1350.

BEDWORTH *All Saints*   SP 361869

Only the 15th century west tower survived the rebuilding of 1888-90.

BENTLEY *Dedication Unknown*   SP 275945

In a field is the east wall of a chapel with a 15th century window.

BERKSWELL *St John The Baptist*   SP 244791

Berkswell has one of the most interesting and complete medieval churches
in Warwickshire. The chancel is a fine Norman structure of c1170-80 with
shafted round headed windows and unusual semi-circular buttresses. Two
stairs set either side of the chancel arch lead down to a large crypt
vaulted in two bays. To the west, below the eastern part of the nave,
is a very unusual octagonal second crypt, also Norman. The arrangement
of the north arcade with a wide 14th century arch east of two Norman
arches suggests that the church originally had transepts removed in the
late 13th century when the south aisle, with a regular three bay arcade,
was built. The north aisle was rebuilt shortly after, and a short chapel
added beyond it beside the chancel. Chapel and aisle were again rebuilt
in the 15th century, the probable period of the unbuttressed west tower,
The clerestory may be later still. The south doorway is a reset Norman
piece now covered by a remarkable timber porch with a jettied upper room
with closely set studding. No medieval monuments survive but there are
15th century screens, some later box pews, and a gallery.

BICKENHILL *St Peter*   SP 189824

The mid 12th century north aisle probably originally formed the nave,
Of the same era are the three western bays of the arcade. The doorway,
buttresses, and windows of the aisle are 14th century. The arcade east
bay, the north chapel with a wide arch towards the chancel, and the west
tower are 15th century. The 14th century chancel and the south wall of
the present nave were mostly rebuilt in 1887. There is a 17th century
communion rail, and in the aisle east end is a screen which seems to have
originally been behind the high altar with a vestry behind.

Bidford
-On-Avon
Church

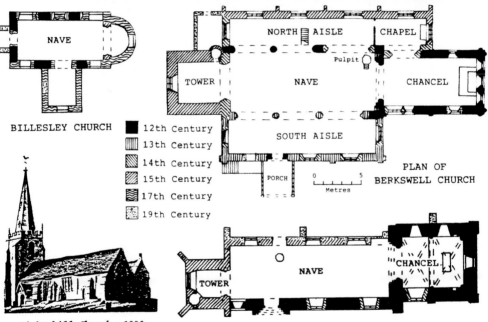

BILLESLEY CHURCH

- ■ 12th Century
- ▥ 13th Century
- ▧ 14th Century
- ▨ 15th Century
- ▧ 17th Century
- ▨ 19th Century

NAVE

TOWER | NAVE | CHANCEL

NORTH AISLE   CHAPEL

Pulpit

SOUTH AISLE

PORCH

0   5
Metres

PLAN OF
BERKSWELL CHURCH

Bickenhill Church c1820

TOWER

NAVE

CHANCEL

PLAN OF BEAUDESERT CHURCH

BIDFORD-ON-AVON *St Laurence*   SP 101518

The chancel has 14th century masonry but the windows are of 1886-9, and
the nave and aisles are all of 1835, the probable date of the battlements
on the 15th century tower. There is a bust to Lady Skipwith, d1655.

BILLESLEY *All Saints*   SP 148568

When the church was rebuilt in 1692 it gained an east apse and a family
pew on the south side, but it retains Norman masonry with a blocked
north doorway and some windows, whilst on the west wall is a sculptured
12th century Christ, possibly once part of a Harrowing of Hell.

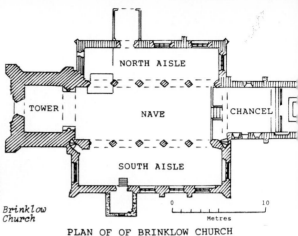

Brinklow Church

PLAN OF OF BRINKLOW CHURCH

BILTON *St Mark*   SP 487739

The south porch and north aisle are additions of 1873, but the chancel as wide as the nave with a large ogee-headed Easter Sepulchre, the south aisle, and west tower are mostly 14th century. The sedilia and piscina are much restored. The chancel north window has fragments of old glass. The font is probably 14th century. The organ case of 1635 is from St John's College at Cambridge, and the late 17th century communion rail is from Great St Mary's Church at Cambridge.

BINTON *St Peter*   SP 144542

The church of 1875 has inside a Jacobean font cover and a dug-out chest.

BIRDINGBURY *St Leonard*   SP 433686

The apse and much else is of 1873 but the building was originally 18th century. The boxpews, font, and pulpit with marquetry are all original.

BIRMINGHAM *St Martin*   SP 074866

By the end of the 13th century a major church stood here with north and south aisles corresponding to the existing ones, and a NW tower with a spire. Of it there remain only the crypt below the west end of the south aisle (another below the nave is now filled in), and part of the inner walling of the tower. By 1690 the soft sandstone walling had crumbled away to the point where it was necessary to encase the church in brick. The spire needed partial rebuilding in 1781, and repair again in 1853, and then in 1873-5 the very neglected church was rebuilt on the original footings, but with added transepts, and an extended east end. Further rebuilding, and the addition of parish rooms, was undertaken after the church was bombed in 1941. Reset in the north transept are the damaged effigies thought to be of Sir William de Birmingham, c1325, and Sir Fulke de Birmingham, c1370. The effigy in the north chapel may be Sir John de Birmingham, c1400, and there is also a priest of c1500.

BIRMINGHAM *St Phillip*   SP 070870

This fine classical style church set in a wide close was designed by Thomas Archer in 1709, mostly built by 1715, and finished in 1725. It became the cathedral of a new diocese in 1905. It has an aisled nave, a west tower flanked by vestibules containing the stairs to galleries, and a chancel flanked by vestries. The church was refaced in 1864-9, a new east end and vestries were added in 1883-4, and in 1958-9 the tower was refaced. The earliest of the many monuments dates from 1761. Most notable of the furnishings is the organ case of 1715.

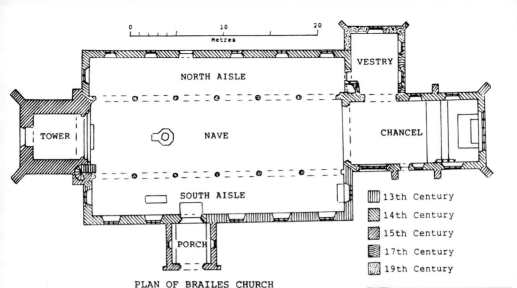

NORTH AISLE

VESTRY

TOWER

NAVE

CHANCEL

SOUTH AISLE

PORCH

▥	13th Century
▨	14th Century
▧	15th Century
▤	17th Century
▦	19th Century

PLAN OF BRAILES CHURCH

BISHOP'S TACHBROOK *St Chad*   SP 414614

The chancel was rebuilt in 1855 except for the north
wall with Norman windows. Also Norman are the reset
doorway in the late 14th century north aisle and the
window head above the early 14th century south aisle
east window. The tower is of c1400. The Wagstaffes
have several monuments, notably Comb, d1668, John,
d1681, and Sir Thomas, d1708. At Chapel Hill Farm to
the NE are remains of a two-celled chapel.

BOURTON-ON-DUNSMORE *St Peter*   SP 436704

Most of the exterior is of c1840. Parts of the south
aisle and arcade, the north transept arch, the font,
and some of the chancel windows are 14th century. The
pulpit is a two decker. There are box pews, a female
effigy of c1300, and a Jacobean communion rail.

BRAILES *St George*   SP 316394

The large church has a high 15th century west tower.
The south aisle with a triple moulded doorway and a
corbel table of monsters and heads is 13th century.
The chancel, with proper seats with stone arms for the
sedilia, north aisle, and clerestory are 14th century.
Several windows and the north arcade are restored. A
14th century font displays eight tracery types. There
is a defaced 15th century effigy on a tomb chest and
there is a tablet to Richard Davies, d1639. The vestry
may be 17th century. It has one reset older window.

BRINKLOW *St John The Baptist*   SP 437796

Parts of the very restored chancel and north aisle are
13th century. The rest is all 15th century with a big
west tower with panelling and niches on the clasping
buttresses, an aisled nave of five bays, and a timber
north porch and contemporary font. There are a few
fragments of old glass with birds set in roundels.

Brailes Church

23

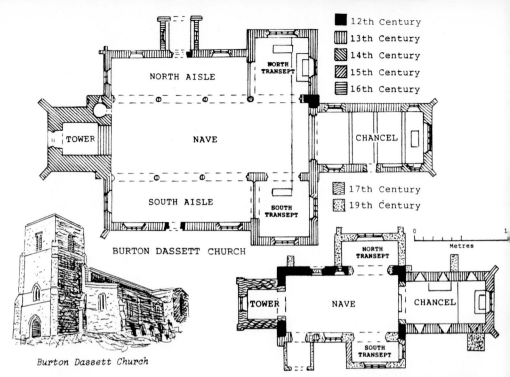

Legend:
- 12th Century
- 13th Century
- 14th Century
- 15th Century
- 16th Century
- 17th Century
- 19th Century

BURTON DASSETT CHURCH

Burton Dassett Church

PLAN OF BUDBROOKE CHURCH

BROWNSOVER *St Michael*   SP 508774

The 13th century chancel has paired south lancets and a 15th century
east window. The nave was mostly rebuilt in 1877 but retains a doorway
and two reset north windows of c1300. The 18th century Flemish pulpit
has a medallion of Christ in profile. Panelling behind it is medieval
and later woodwork of note are the screen dado and parts of the organ.

BUBBENHALL *St Giles*   SP 360725

The tower and nave are late 13th century, the arch between them having
green men head corbels. The north doorway is slightly later, whilst the
chancel, with lancets, may be earlier. In the 19th century the east wall
was rebuilt and the narrow chancel arch moved slightly eastwards. It was
given flanking arches, perhaps ghosts of original altar niches.

BUDBROOK *St Michael*   SP 258656

The nave has a Norman north doorway with one order of shafts and a hood
mould decorated with billets. The chancel has 13th century lancets. The
tower is mostly or entirely of 1668, the year that is engraved upon it.
The north transept is of 1838. The south transept is probably Victorian
too but replaces a 13th century south aisle of which there are traces of
the arcade. There is a monument to Rouland, Baron Dormer of Wing, d1712.

BULKINGTON *St James*   SP 391868

The five bay south and north arcades are early and late 13th century
respectively. The south aisle has one unrestored window with Y-tracery.
The north aisle is wider and has a long squint looking into the 14th
century chancel. The tower is probably late 14th century. Only the south
side has a clerestory, which is of 15th century date. The marble font
and two Hayward monuments are of the end of the 18th century.

Butlers
Marston
Church

BURMINGTON *St Barnabas & St Nicholas*   SP 264379

The chancel arch with a trumpet scallop capital dates the chancel c1200.
The nave masonry is said to be late 17th century but the west end, with
a tiny NW turret and the porch and vestry are 19th century.

BURTON DASSETT *All Saints*   SP 398515

This is a large and little restored church lying on a hill away from any
village. Of the Norman nave there remain the east quoins and two reset
doorways. There are aisles and transepts of the 13th century with four
arches on each side, although on the south a section of wall divides the
transept arch from the rest. The north arcade capitals have nailhead and
creatures walk on the abacus. The chancel of c1300 has windows with Y-
and intersecting tracery. Several windows around the church are of the
15th century, and the tower is 14th century. There are old tiles and a
few benches with poppy heads. The tomb chest in a recess in the north
transept has the indent of former brasses of Peter Temple, d1577, and
his wife. In the south transept is a tomb chest of John Swain, 1658, and
his wife Anne, d1677. Ruins of a chapel-of-ease lie at Northend 1km NW.

BURTON HASTINGS *St Botolph*   SP 410899

The west tower, the nave with a fine window in each side wall and stair
to the roodloft in the NE corner, and the chancel are all 15th century.
Only the font of c1300 is earlier. It has trefoiled arches and rosettes.

BUTLERS MARSTON *St Peter & St Paul*   SP 321500

The south aisle has a three bay Late Norman arcade and a 17th century
doorway and windows. The west tower and font are 15th century, and the
pulpit is Jacobean. The rest is Victorian except some chancel walling.

CALDECOTE *St Theobald & St Chad*   SP 348951

The dedication to St Theobald is a great rarity, only three being known
in England. The nave and chancel are of c1280-1300 but were restored in
the 1850s when the vestry, organ recess, and porch were added, so that
the fragments of old glass and the south door with long scroll hinges
are now the only ancient features of much interest.

CASTLE BROMWICH *St Mary & St Margaret*   SP 143899

During the restoration of 1891-3 it was discovered that the church built
in 1726-31 by Thomas White was in fact only a remodelling of a medieval
timber framed building. White encased the four arcade posts on each side,
ceiled off the open roof and put up high parapets and a big west tower.
His walls are of brick with segmental headed windows. The furnishings,
including a three decker pulpit, are mostly of the 18th century.

CHADSHUNT *All Saints*   SP 350530

The nave has two Norman doorways, a 13th century twin lancet, one 14th century window, and a roof with tie-beams and king-posts. The tower may be 17th century. The chancel and the wrought iron communion rail are 18th century, and so probably is the north chapel in which are a family pew and some Italian glass dated 1558. The monument of Michael Askel, dated 1713, has seated putti. The Norman font has intersecting arches.

CHARLECOTE *St Leonard*   SP 263565

In the family chapel of the church of 1851-3 are the recumbent effigies on tomb chests of three Sir Thomas Lucys, d1600, 1605, and 1640, with their wives.

Coleshill Font

CHERINGTON *St John The Baptist*   SP 292364

There are triple mid 13th century lancet windows in the chancel, **nave**, and north aisle, and the two bay arcade goes with them, although the apparently matching north aisle north windows are actually 18th century. Slightly earlier and later respectively are the south doorway of c1210, and the west tower of c1290, whilst the porch is of c1320. A tomb chest and effigy of a 14th century civilian is squeezed into the nave wall to the east of the arcade respond. The tower seems to have been remodelled in the late 15th century when a clerestory was built and one new window inserted in the nave. Collected together by a mid 18th century rector is the collection of stained glass from the 14th century to the 18th.

CHESTERTON *St Giles*   SP 357583

The west tower is partly or wholly of c1600. The long nave is the same width as the chancel. It has a 13th century north doorway, a fine south doorway of c1320 with ballflowers, and south windows and porch probably of the early 16th century. The nave has a low pitched roof with moulded tie-beams. The fragmentary Adoration of The Magi is likely to be from a reredos of c1400. One window has some old glass. There are recumbent effigies of Humphrey Peyto, d1585, and his wife, a reredos type monument of 1639 to William Peyto and busts of Edward Peyto, d1643, and his wife.

CHILVERS COTON *All Saints*   SP 364907

Only the 15th century west tower has survived 19th century rebuilding and restoration after damage sustained during the Second World War.

CHURCH LAWFORD *St Peter*   SP 454764

The rebuilding of 1872 has left only the 14th century four bay arcade, a south doorway of c1210, an old font, the Jabobean pulpit, an 18th century communion rail and a few architectural fragments lying below the tower.

CHURCHOVER *Holy Trinity*   SP 511808

The church was mostly rebuilt in 1896-7, but the south doorway is partly 13th century, the south arcade is of c1300, and the west tower is 15th century, although the parapet is later and the spire was rebuilt in 1885. The Norman font is flowerpot shaped and has a rope moulding. Reset in the south aisle west wall is a Norman capital. There are monuments with kneeling figures of Robert Price, d1595, and Charles Dixwell, d1641.

CLAVERDON *St Michael*   SP 198646

Rebuildings of 1830 and 1877 have left only the 15th century west tower, the 14th century chancel arch, and Thomas Spencer's monument of c1600.

Tomb at Cherington

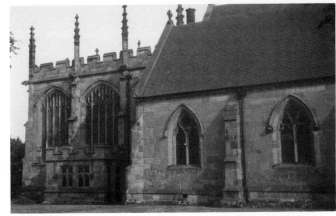

Coleshill Church

CLIFFORD CHAMBERS *St Helen* SP 199522

Norman are the pillar piscina and the nave masonry
and north and south doorways. The latter has columns
with scallop capitals. The tower may be 15th century
like several of the windows, although its masonry may
be older. The chancel and vestries are Victorian but
reset in the latter is a 13th century low side window.
There are fragments of old glass, a Jacobean pulpit,
a late 17th century communion rail, and a brass to
Sir Henry Rainsford, d1622, and his wife and family.

CLIFTON-ON-DUNSMORE *St Mary* SP 532764

The 13th century chancel has paired lancets in the
side walls and a triple lancet to the east. Parts of
the south arcade are also 13th century. The aisle was
rebuilt wider in c1300 and soon afterwards the tower
and north aisle were added. The upper stage of the
tower is probably 16th century and once had a spire.
The chancel arch and some of the south aisle features
are Victorian. A heart burial in a casket below the
chancel was found in 1894. There is a large tablet to
Sir Orlando Bridgeman, d1721.

COLESHILL *St Peter & St Paul* SP 202890

This is a large 14th and 15th century church but much
of the exterior has been renewed, especially on the
south side. The eastern four bays of both arcades are
14th century. The large tower with a lofty spire was
begun c1385 and then c1400 the nave was joined up to
it with three new bays. The wide 15th century chancel
has five light side windows and one of seven lights
to the east. Remains of sedilia show the floor was
originally lower. There is a very fine 12th century
font with figures in arcading and a Crucifixion with
the Virgin and St John. Each aisle contains an early
14th century effigy of a knight whilst the chancel
contains brasses of Vicar William Abell, d1500, Alice
Clifton, d1506, and Sir John Fenton, d1586. There are
alabaster effigies of Simon Digby, d1520, John Digby,
d1558, and Sir George Digby, d1586, with their wives
on tomb chests. On another tomb chest is an incised
slab depicting Reginald Digby, d1549, and his wife,
and there are monuments without effigies to the 1st
and 2nd Lords Digby, d1642 and 1672 respectively.

The Tower, Coleshill Church

27

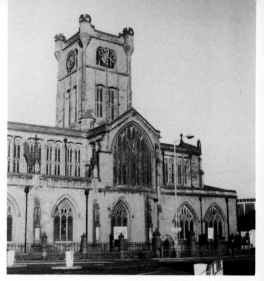

Holy
Trinity
Church,
Coventry

St John's
Church,
Coventry

COMPTON WYNIATES *Dedication Unknown*   SP 330419

Except for an older tower the chapel north of the house is of the 1660s.
It has a font of that period, box pews, and an 18th century communion
rail. There are 17 hatchments of the late 17th and early 18th centuries.
There is a tablet to Sir William Compton, d1663. The effigies of a late
15th century lady, two 16th century knights, and two late 16th century
ladies were probably vandalised by Parliamentary troops in the Civil War.

CORLEY *Dedication Unknown*   SP 302851

The nave has two Norman windows with internal roll mouldings and a south
doorway with one order of shafts with spiral volutes on the capitals and
saltire crosses on the tympanum. The neo Norman windows are of 1893.
The Late Norman north aisle has a two bay arcade with scallop capitals
and traces of a painting of St Christopher on the 14th century northern
wall. The ashlar faced chancel is of c1300, and the vestry is of 1967.

COUGHTON *St Peter*   SP 084606

The aisled nave with three bay arcades and a clerestory and a west tower
are late 15th century although the tower top is rather later. Of c1500-
20 are the chancel with two bay chapels which have windows with uncusped
lights. The north chapel has a brick turret which gave access to a rood
loft. The loft has gone but the screens remain. Linenfold panels of the
1520s appear on the pulpit, reredos, and stalls. There is a bread dole
board of 1717. Part of the font is 15th century. The chapel windows have
some old glass. In the middle of the nave lies the tomb of Sir Robert
Throckmorton who died in the Holy Land in 1518 leaving money in his will
for the Doom in stained glass in the east window, the Seven Sacrements
in the north chapel windows and the Seven Acts of Mercy in the south
chapel. There are numerous other Throckmorton monuments, including the
brasses of Sir George, d1533 and his wife on a tomb chest, a plain tomb
chest of Sir Robert, d1570, and recumbent effigies under a six poster
canopy of Sir John, 1580, and his wife with kneeling children alongside.
A 17th century column and sundial lie on the churchyard crossbase.

COVENTRY *Christchurch*   SP 334787

This very fine octagonal steeple and spire of c1350 set upon the lofty
arches of the narrow crossing of the Franciscan Friary church was used
as the chancel of a parish church built in 1830-2, and destroyed by a
bomb in 1940. Recently the crossing space has been made into a shop.

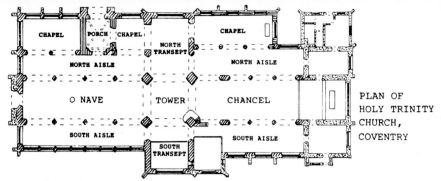

PLAN OF
HOLY TRINITY
CHURCH,
COVENTRY

COVENTRY *Holy Trinity*

SP 335790

This church served the half of the city belonging to the Priory. It was
a substantial building large enough to hold its own visually against St
Michael's close to the SE, and the huge Priory Church to the north. It
has an aisled nave of four bays, a crossing tower with a fine spire,
and transepts. These parts are 15th century in their present form but
all probably existed by the end of the 13th century. Certainly the north
porch surviving from then belonged to a very spacious building. A chapel
between the porch and the north transept is thought to have been that
of St Thomas founded by the Dyers Guild in 1296. West of the porch is a
15th or 16th century chapel. From 1391 onwards the chancel was rebuilt
with four bay arcades, being lengthened eastwards. The Marley Chapel
beyond the north chancel aisle was added in 1537. The south transept was
built over a public passageway of which a blocked archway can be seen.
The church has been heavily restored several times. The whole east end
and vestries are 18th and 19th century work, and much of the remainder
was refaced externally in the 1840s. An exception is the fine series of
eight windows on the south side without walling or buttressing between.

There are several noteworthy furnishings including a medieval stone
pulpit built as part of the SE crossing pier, a 15th century font, stalls
from the Whitefriars' Church with curious carvings on the miserichords,
and an ancient brass lectern with an eagle top. There are also fragments
of old glass and a rather blackened painting of the Last Judgement over
the west crossing arch. Grouped in the NW chapel are a brass depicting
John Whithead, d1600, with his wives kneeling on either side, busts of
John Bohun, d1691, and his family, and a brass indent on a tomb chest.

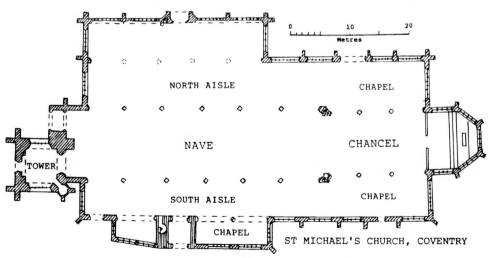

ST MICHAEL'S CHURCH, COVENTRY

COVENTRY *St John The Baptist*   SP 331790

This church was built to serve a college founded by Edward II's widow
Queen Isabella in the 1340s. The outer walls of the nave are original,
but the remainder dates from a 15th century remodelling when a central
tower was built with shallow transepts on either side, with three bay
arcades for the nave, and two bay arcades between the chancel and its
chapels. The eastern part of the north chapel was later walled off to
form a vestry, but there is an irregularly shaped 15th century vestry
to the north of it. The whole building is very irregularly planned. On
the corners of the tower at the top are 19th century bartizans.

COVENTRY *St Michael*   SP 337790

The church was first established in the early 12th century to serve the
southern half of the city held by the Earl of Chester. It grew to be
one of the three largest English parish churches, and in 1918 was made
a cathedral. Except for the very fortunate survival of the tower and
spire the church was gutted by a bombing raid in November 1940, and in
the 1950s a new cathedral designed by Sir Basil Spence was erected to
north, the old church being left ruinous as a war memorial.
    The south porch is 13th century but the remainder was rebuilt or
added in various stages between the 1370s and the 1530s and is in what
is known as the Perpendicular style. The south aisle must represent the
original 13th century layout. South of it, left and right of the porch,
are the Dyers' and Cappers' chapels. After the tower was begun c1371
(it and the 90m high spire were only finished in the 1430s) the nave was
widened into the space of a former north aisle, so leaving the tower
offset to the south with space for a west porch to the north of it. The
new nave had six wide bays and a wide new north aisle, the east end of
which was built over a crypt of c1300 (now a shop) which lay below the
former north transept. Beyond the north aisle an outer aisle was later
added with a shallow porch in the middle. On either side lay the Smiths'
and Girdlers' guild chapels. East of the widened nave a new chancel was
constructed with three bay arcades opening to the Drapers' and Mercers'
chapels respectively. It ended in a polygonal apse, a rarity in English
parochial churches. The 19th century vestries added around the apse are
still in use. The outer walls of the rest all stand high but the main
arcades have gone, their piers having been cracked by the fire.

*Spire of
Holy Trinity
Coventry*

*Apse, St
Michael,
Coventry*

Curdworth Church

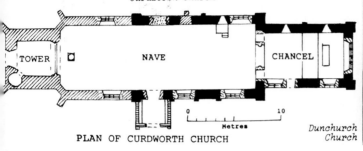

| TOWER | NAVE | CHANCEL |

0   10

Metres

PLAN OF CURDWORTH CHURCH

Dunchurch Church

CUBBINGTON *St Mary*   SP 345685

The three bay south arcade is Norman although the aisle seems to have been rebuilt c1300. The tower with clasping buttresses is Late Norman, but has two 13th century lancets on the north side at the bell stage. The 14th century chancel with ogee headed sedilia and Easter Sepulchre is as long and wide as the nave. The latter has a tie-beam roof having collar-beams and queen-posts. The chancel arch is comparatively narrow. The north aisle is late 14th or early 15th century. The arcade has been rebuilt. There is a tablet to Captain Murcott, d1703 in a shipwreck.

CURDWORTH *St Nicholas*   SP 177928

Nave and chancel and the arch between them with waterleaf capitals and keeled rolls are of c1180-90. There are traces of the windows and two doorways plus many pilaster buttresses. Flanking the chancel arch are smaller openings, although only that on the south is medieval. There are 13th century patterns painted on the window reveals. The font also is Norman with a lamb, atlas, two pairs of men, a winged monster, etc. The four light east window has intersecting tracery of c1300. The nave was later extended westwards to meet up with the 15th century tower.

DORSINGTON *St Peter*   SP 133496

The present church of red and yellow brick with thin west towers is of 1758 but may be on older foundations. The pulpit has early and late 17th century panels and the font bowl is medieval with a base of the 1660s.

DUNCHURCH *St Peter*   SP 486713

The chancel is late 13th century but is much restored. A renewed arcade of two bays opens to a north chapel, entirely rebuilt except a reset window of c1300. A 19th century vestry has been added against the south aisle which has a three bay 14th century arcade. The piers are built on Norman bases so there was an earlier, narrower, aisle here. The north aisle and tower are late 14th or early 15th century. The tower has twin two light transomed bell openings, a top frieze of quatrefoils and a high arch to the nave. There are traceried panels of late medieval date from a former pulpit or bench bends.

31

Edgbaston
Church

Fillongley
Church

EARLSDON *St Barbara*   SP 321780

Inside the brick church of 1930-1 is a big decorated font of 1661.

EDGBASTON *St Bartholomew*   SP 057848

Facing Church Road are the outer wall of the narrow north aisle, porch, and vestry, all late medieval, as is the lower part of the tower. The church was badly damaged in the Civil War. A new south aisle and west porch were built in 1856, and an outer south aisle, a new east end, and new arcades were built in 1885-9. Fixed on the refaced inner side of the north aisle wall are several monuments to the Gough family.

ETTINGTON *Holy Trinity*   SP 248473

The medieval church beside Ettington Park was partly dismantled after a new church was built in the village in the 1790s. That in turn was taken down except the tower when a new church was built beside it in 1902-3. The old church had 13th century transepts but little remains of either, the north side having all gone save the three bay 14th century arcade and aisle west wall, and the south transept having been remodelled in 1875 as a mortuary chapel for the Shirleys. Within it are defaced recumbent effigies of Ralph Shirley, d1327, and his wife, an effigy of Dame Frances Freckleton, d1633, with a canopy on four posts, and effigies of 1775 of the Earl and Countess Ferrers, plus other monuments. The chancel south wall has one 14th century window and one 15th century one. The nave has a 14th century south doorway and a big plain mullioned window, perhaps 17th century. Rather more complete is the tower of c1190-1200 with big clasping pilaster buttresses. A south window pierces a mid-wall pilaster.

EXHALL *St Giles*   SP 103551

The nave has a Norman north doorway, and the chancel has 13th century lancets. On the south side is a fine window of c1320 with ballflowers.

EXHALL *St Giles*   SP 341850

The south aisle and arcades are of 1842 and the vestry is of 1885, but the north aisle is partly of 1609, the date over one north window. The west tower is 15th century. The chancel of c1300 has an east window with intersecting tracery.

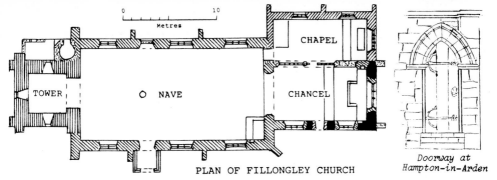

PLAN OF FILLONGLEY CHURCH

Doorway at Hampton-in-Arden

FARNBOROUGH *St Botolph*　　　　　　　　　　SP 434495

Prominent from the north are the wide aisle and spire of 1875. The tower, porch, and chancel are all early 14th century but the outer order of the chancel arch and the south doorway with chevrons on the arch and a fish scale patterned tympanum are late 12th century. There are a head of an effigy of a knight of c1200, a brass inscription to Mary Wagstaffe, 1667, and tablets to Jeremiah Hall, d1711, and William Holbech, d1777.

FENNY COMPTON *St Peter & St Clare*　　　　　SP 417522

Only one other English church is dedicated to St Clare. The chancel and the north aisle with its five bay arcade and porch are of the first half of the 14th century; the tower is of the end of the century. The south aisle is of 1879. The clerestory is 15th century. The communion rail is 17th century. The pulpit is contemporary with it or just a little later.

FILLONGLEY *St Mary & All Saints*　　　　　　SP 281873

The chancel retains some Norman masonry with traces of the east windows. The long nave was rebuilt wider c1300 when the chancel was given new windows. Of the 15th century are the upper parts of the 13th century west tower, the nave clerestory, and the two bay north chapel with its ceiling of moulded beams with bosses and glass depicting the builder and his family. There are also fragments of 14th century glass, a font either of the 15th or 17th centuries, and an architectural monument of 1725 to a Mrs Daniel and her daughter. The tracery panels of the stall front and prayer desk are probably made from former bench ends.

FOLESHILL *St Laurence*　　　　　　　　　　　SP 333825

The west tower, the north aisle, and the responds of the north arcade are 15th century, but the church was mostly rebuilt after the village became a Coventry suburb. The brick NE vestry is dated 1812, the wide south aisle is of 1801, the chancel is Victorian, and the spacious south chapel is of 1927. The font with chevron bands is Norman.

FRANKTON *St Nicholas*　　　　　　　　　　　SP 424702

The short west tower is 13th century with a 15th century top. The south arcade responds are of c1300-20 but the features of the aisle and the chancel which have survived the heavy restoration of 1872 are c1360-90.

GAYDON *St Giles*　　　　　　　　　　　　　　SP 364540

Only the south doorway has survived the rebuilding of 1852.

GRANDBOROUGH *St Peter*　　　　　　　　　　SP 493670

The chancel, with intersecting tracery in the east window, is as large as the nave, which has aisles with four bay arcades and windows with Y-tracery and reticulation. All this is of c1300-40, but the tower and spire are about two generations later. The communion rail is Georgian.

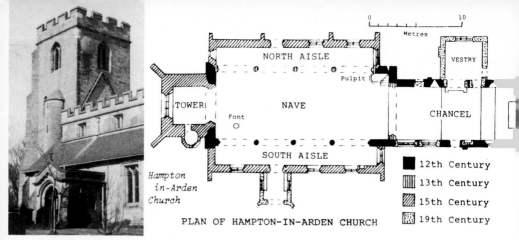

PLAN OF HAMPTON-IN-ARDEN CHURCH

NORTH AISLE

VESTRY

TOWER

NAVE

Font

Pulpit

CHANCEL

SOUTH AISLE

Hampton
in-Arden
Church

0   10
Metres

■ 12th Century
▥ 13th Century
▨ 15th Century
▩ 19th Century

GREAT ALNE *St Mary Magdalene*   SP 117595

The chancel has a 13th century lancet and doorway. The nave has one 15th
century north window but is mostly of 1837 and 1860 when a short aisle
was added. There is a large brick vestry beside the chancel.

GRENDON *All Saints*   SK 287009

The chancel with lancets and the north aisle with nailhead decoration on
the arcade are 13th century. The chancel arch and the south aisle with
a three bay arcade on quatrefoil shaped piers are 14th century. The west
tower and probably also the vestry are of 1845. The font is Georgian and
there is a fine Jacobean pulpit. The tower screen has come from St Mary
at Stafford. Between the south chapel and aisle is a late 17th century
screen. The communion rail is late 17th century and the reredos is c1740.
The earliest of numerous monuments to the Chetwynds of Pooley Hall are
an incised slab to Margaret, d1539, and a tablet to John, d1593. There
is also an alabaster effigy of an unknown 15th century lady.

GUY'S CLIFFE   SP 294668

Beside the ruined house is a chapel built by Richard ¬eauchamp, Earl of
Warwick in the 1420s. A tower was added in 1450. The interior is two-
naved and has an 18th century plaster vault and a huge effigy of St Guy
carved out of the native sandstone against which the chapel is built.

HALFORD *St Mary*   SP 259457

The north doorway of c1140 has a fine tympanum depicting a seated angel.
it is similar in style to the work of the Herefordshire School. Reset
in the 13th century south aisle with a tower at its west end is another
Norman doorway. The aisle, chancel, and nave north side were mostly all
rebuilt in the 1860s and 1880s. The font is medieval and has a cover with
five bishop's heads on the top knob, probably early 16th century work.
Within the church are two firehooks used to pull off burning thatch.

HAMPTON-IN-ARDEN *St Mary & St Bartholomew*   SP 202808

The Norman nave and chancel are both quite long. They are not in axis
with each other, probably as a result of an earlier chancel being made
wider to the south when it was rebuilt and lengthened. The south arcade
of four bays is of c1170-80, while the north arcade and chancel are of
the 1230s. The narrow aisles were rebuilt on the old foundations in the
15th century when the west tower was added. The tower had a spire which
fell in 1643. The embattled clerestory may be as late as the middle of
the 16th century. The half figure with a shield under a pointed arch may
commemorate a late 13th century heart burial. There is a small brass of
a man of c1500 in civilian costume.

34

Tympanum at Halford

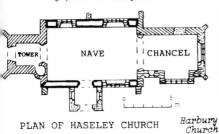

PLAN OF HASELEY CHURCH

TOWER   NAVE   CHANCEL

Harbury Church

HANDSWORTH St Mary   SP 056904

Handsworth has a large sprawling church with a long nave, south aisle,
south porch, and inner and outer north aisles of the 1870s, a transept
with a vestry east of it of the 1820s, and on the chancel south side is
a chapel of 1826 housing the monument of the inventor James Watt. Of a
smaller but still substantial medieval church there remains a Late Norman
tower at the east end of the south aisle, with a 15th century top stage
and stair turret, some 14th century masonry in the chancel, and most of
the 16th century north chapel, with an older doorway at the west end of
its north wall. As well as several 19th century monuments there are two
effigies on a tomb chest in the north chapel of William Wyrley, d1561,
and his wife, fragments of an incised slab to Thomas Wyrley and his
wife, d1598, and in the south aisle is a 16th century effigy of a corpse
in a burial shroud.

HARBORNE St Peter   SP 028839

The church was entirely rebuilt in 1867 except for the medieval tower.

HARBOROUGH MAGNA All Saints   SP 476793

The wide north aisle with ogee heads to the blocked doorway and a tomb
recess, and a two bay arcade with a quatrefoil pier, is of c1300. The arch
to the tower is 15th century, the south arcade dates from c1300, and the
chancel arch is late 13th century. These parts were mostly rebuilt 1869.

HARBURY All Saints   SP 370600

The chancel has a 13th century lancet on each side, the south one having
a low side window. The three bay south arcade and SW tower are late 13th
century, although the aisle seems to have been widened shortly after.
It has been much restored and the north aisle is all of 1873. The tower
has an embattled brick top stage probably of c1830. The small font and
communion rail are 18th century.

HASELEY St Mary   SP 238680

The 15th century west tower has some old glass in the west window. Apart
from the south doorway of c1200 the nave and chancel features are mostly
17th century with plain mullioned windows and a projection with a cross
gable in the chancel which houses a tomb chest with brasses of Clement
Throckmorton, d1573, and his wife. The interior is comparatively little
restored. It has a ceiled wagon roof, box pews, and a 15th century font.

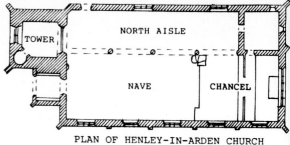

PLAN OF HENLEY-IN-ARDEN CHURCH

0 _____ 10
m

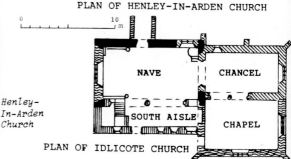

Henley-In-Arden Church

PLAN OF IDLICOTE CHURCH

HASELOR *St Mary Magdalene & All Saints*   SP 125579

The tower is said to be Norman although its features are 14th century. The blocked two bay arcade of a former north chapel is of c1190, and the three western arches of the south arcade are probably contemporary. The eastern arch is 13th century. Except for the doorway the aisle features have been renewed, as has the north wall, with a projecting mausoleum. The chancel has Jacobean panelling, one 14th century window and traces of a doorway which must have led to a vestry east of the former chapel.

HATTON *Holy Trinity*   SP 236673

The rebuilding of 1880 left only the 15th century west tower which has in the west window twelve stained glass half figures from a German 16th century Tree of Jesse. There are numerous tablets of late date.

HENLEY-IN-ARDEN *St John The Baptist*   SP 153661

This church is squeezed into a corner site and is very close to that of Beaudesert. It is all late 15th century and has a nave and chancel in one and a north aisle with a tower to the west and a vestry to the east. The roofs and pulpit are original. A doorway has king and queen headstops.

HILLMORTON *St John The Baptist*   SP 536744

The red ashlar west tower, the nave and aisles with five bay arcades, and the chancel are mostly of c1300 although the east window with some intersecting tracery typical of that date is actually dated 1640. Some windows appear late medieval, those on the south having a thick middle mullion which may be a later alteration, and the clerestory is probably mid 16th century. The nave has a roof of tie-beams on arched braces. The pulpit, box pews and west gallery are all 18th century. There is a fine early 14th century female effigy, a good early 15th century brass of a lady, and defaced effigies of a 14th century knight and priest.

HONILEY *St John The Baptist*   SP 245722

The white stone church of 1723 has a Baroque west tower with a smaller top stage joined on with eight volutes, a nave still having original box pews, west gallery and pulpit, and an apse with marble internal pilasters. A niche in one tower arch respond forms the font.

36

HONINGTON *All Saints*   SP 262427

The church lies by the hall and was rebuilt as a nave and aisles of four
bays with Tuscan columns and a shallow segmental plaster vault, and an
apse in the 1680s, although the west tower survives from c1270-1300. The
font, pulpit, communion rail, stalls and benches are all of the time of
the rebuilding. There is a fine marble monument to Sir Henry Parker,
d1713, and his son Hugh, d1712. The earliest of several tablets to the
Townsends is that to Joseph, d1763.

HUNNINGHAM *St Margaret*   SP 373672

The wide north aisle is of 1868-71 except for the blocked north doorway
of c1200. The nave west lancet pierces a buttress. The south doorway
and low side window are late medieval. The rest is mostly Victorian.

IDLICOTE *St James*   SP 283442

The nave north doorway is of c1200. The narrow south aisle with a two
bay arcade is late 13th century, and the chancel is of c1300. The west
window and much of the west wall go with the Underhill Chapel added in
the late 17th century and having a two bay arcade with a Tuscan column
towards the chancel. Of the same period are the ogee-shaped font cover,
the pulpit and tester, and a communion rail. The remnants of a screen
are earlier. The main altar communion rail is 18th century. The chapel
windows are Victorian. Within it are a number of tablets.

ILMINGTON *St Mary*   SP 210435

The nave is essentially Norman, with two original doorways, two small
windows and a double stepped chancel arch. The west tower of c1200 has
clasping and mid-wall pilasters, the latter with lancets in them, but
the tower arch may be considerably later. The 13th century chancel has
lancets and niches with pointed arches inside at the west end. Transepts
were added in the 15th century. The north transept lies on the site of
a 13th century chapel, parts of the arcade of which were reused. The
south transept has been much restored but retains part of a frieze with
a chained bear being baited by a dog. The damaged effigy of a priest of
c1400 below the tower is the only pre-Victorian monument.

Ilmington Church

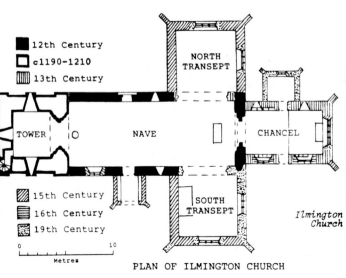

■ 12th Century
□ c1190-1210
▨ 13th Century

▨ 15th Century
▤ 16th Century
▦ 19th Century

0 _____ 10
Metres

PLAN OF ILMINGTON CHURCH

KENILWORTH *St Nicholas*

The western bay of the north porch forms an aisle originally entered from the west as well as north. It is 15th century, like the arcades and the aisle. The south wall and most of the east end is of 1864. The tower is 14th century and has an octagonal upper stage and spire. From the nearby abbey, which the church served as a parochial chapel, are the magnificent Norman doorway, and the assortment of carved stones, including corbels and capitals. The doorway is reset in the tower and has two orders of columns and sunk medallions in the spandrels of the unusual rectangular frame. In the chancel are reset 14th century sedilia. The font bears the date 1664 and has flat scallops and four flowers plus other motifs.

KINETON *St Peter*

SP 335511

The church is built of a toffee coloured stone which crumbles easily and has necessitated total rebuildings in 1755 and 1873-89 except the late 13th century west tower with a splendid moulded west doorway and 15th century openwork battlements, and possibly parts of the arcade. Also medieval are a defaced effigy and the copper processional cross. The tower basement is an unusual tunnel vaulted passage of uncertain date.

KINGSBURY *St Peter & St Paul*

SP 215963

The west tower, aisles, and chancel with sedilia and piscina are mostly of c1300. The arcade arches of that period are supported on piers and responds which are Norman work probably rearranged as the Norman arcade arches could not possibly have been as wide as the present ones are. The transeptal Bracebridge chapel added c1395 has a squint to the chancel and an arch with a green man with a monkey towards the north aisle. The vestry east of the chapel is early 14th century. In the chapel are a slab with a bust in a quatrefoil and two defaced 14th century effigies.

KINGS NEWNHAM *St Laurence*

SP 448773

Only the tower now remains. It has a Norman north window and mullioned two light bellstage openings probably of c1600.

KING'S NORTON *St Nicholas*

SP 049789

King's Norton is a Birmingham suburb still retaining a village layout and atmosphere with a large medieval church adjoining a green. Only the north aisle outer wall, the NE vestry, organ chamber, and some of the chancel features are Victorian. The chancel has 13th century walling, 14th century buttresses and chancel arch, and a reset Norman window. The long wide nave has seven bay arcades with octagonal, circular, and quatrefoil shaped pillars. The north arcade is late 13th century, and the south arcade and wide south aisle are early 14th century. The south porch and west tower and spire are 15th century and the clerestory is of c1659. Until it was rebuilt the north aisle had a series of cross gables. Within it are a worn incised slab probably to Humfrey Toye, a chaplain, d1514, and a wall monument made c1740 to John Middlemore, d1698. Under the tower is a large incised slab to Humfrie Littleton, d1624, and his wife Martha, and effigies of Sir Richard Grevis, d1632.

KINWARTON *St Mary*

SP 106584

The single chamber with clasping east corner buttresses and north lancets is mostly 13th century. Two south windows, one with some old glass, are 14th century, and the west buttresses and windows are 19th century. The weatherboarded turret stands on two posts with bracing forming an arch and two X's, probably 16th or 17th century. A 15th century alabaster panel shows the Virgin in The Temple. The chandelier is 18th century.

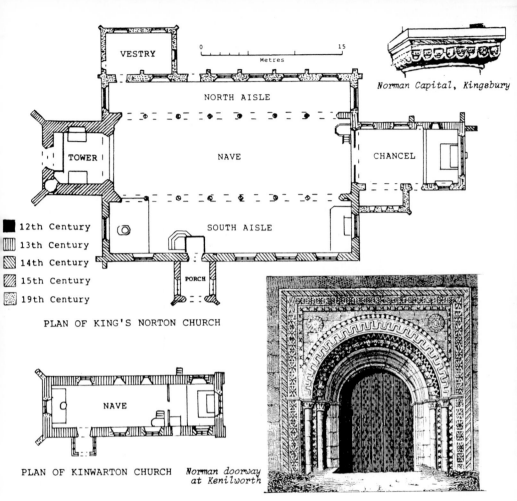

VESTRY

NORTH AISLE

0   15
Metres

Norman Capital, Kingsbury

TOWER

NAVE

CHANCEL

■ 12th Century

▥ 13th Century

▨ 14th Century

▧ 15th Century

▦ 19th Century

SOUTH AISLE

PORCH

PLAN OF KING'S NORTON CHURCH

NAVE

PLAN OF KINWARTON CHURCH   *Norman doorway at Kenilworth*

KNOWLE   *St John The Baptist, St Laurence, & St Anne*   SP 183768

The consecration recorded in 1402, and the founding of a college in 1416 must refer to the building of the present church comprising an aisled five bay nave with an embattled clerestory, a west tower, and a lofty chancel with a subway beneath the east end for the use of processions as the church evidently did not then own the land to the east. Within are two sets of sedilia and piscina of before and after the building of the eastern bay on the subway. The transeptal north chapel is slightly later. Of the same date as the church are the font, screen, and stalls with miserichords carved mostly with foliage. Other features of interest are two dug-out chests, a late 17th century hourglass on the pulpit, and two iron brackets of 1717 carrying a lion and unicorn.

LADBROKE   *All Saints*   SP 414589

The chancel is late 13th century but the sedilia and Easter Sepulchre go with the early 14th century three bay arcades, aisles, porch, and west tower. There is a fine head over the south doorway. One window has some original glass and there is a damaged effigy of a priest. Later only are the spire, three former roof corbels now loose in the porch, and the tablet to William Palmer, d1720, and his wife Mary, d1729.

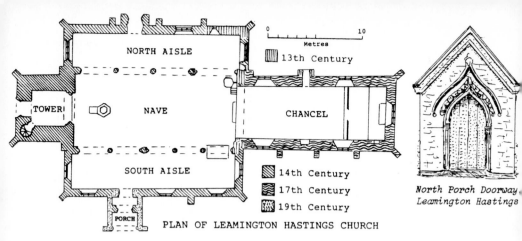

NORTH AISLE

13th Century

| 0 | | | 10 |
Metres

TOWER

NAVE

CHANCEL

SOUTH AISLE

14th Century

17th Century

19th Century

PORCH

PLAN OF LEAMINGTON HASTINGS CHURCH

North Porch Doorway
Leamington Hastings

LAPWORTH *St Mary* SP 164711

Parts of the Norman nave survive including one window above the eastern
pier of the four bay 13th century north arcade. The arches to the aisle
and chancel show the north chapel cannot be much later than c1200 either
although it was remodelled in the 14th and 19th centuries. The chancel
has some 13th century masonry and 14th century windows. The nave west
front with two lancets set in a thick buttressed wall and parts of the
aisles, with traces of former lancets on the south, and the south arcade
are 13th century. The 14th century tower (the spire is slightly later)
was originally detatched until connected to the north aisle in the 19th
century. However, in spite of all these features, the general impression
of the church from outside is 15th century, the clerestory, battlements,
aisle windows and relic chamber projecting to the west over the former
street all being of that date. The relic chamber is reached from the
public passage below by a pair of spiral staircases. The 14th century
font has heads projecting from below it. The stalls include some reset
late medieval panels. In the north chapel are traces of old murals.

LEA MARSTON *St John The Baptist* SP 204927

The much restored nave is of c1300 and there is a 15th century porch.
The chancel and NW tower are all of the 1870s. The earliest of the many
monuments to the Adderleys of Hams Hall is that of Sir Charles, d1682.

Leamington
Hastings
Church

LEAMINGTON HASTINGS *All Saints*   SP 445676

The large chancel is entirely of 1677, the year that appears above the east window. The three eastern arches of the south arcade with nailhead decoration are 13th century. There was continuous building here during the 14th century. First a north transept was added, then the south aisle was rebuilt and lengthened with two further arches, then three further arches were built on the north side and a north aisle created, and last of all a west tower was added. The clerestory windows are 16th or 17th century. The late medieval font is a hexagon with angel busts. There are medieval panels in the pulpit, and a reading desk seems to have been formed from its door. There are monuments with busts of two Sir Thomas Trevors who died in 1656 and 1676 respectively, and the latter's wife.

LIGHTHORNE *St Lawrence*   SP 336560

The church was rebuilt in 1875-6 except for the west tower of 1771. In the NE window is some 17th century heraldic stained glass.

LILLINGTON *St Mary Magdalene*   SP 330672

Though it has 14th century features, the chancel may have Norman walls. The tower is 15th century. The rest is all of 1847, and 1884, etc.

LITTLE COMPTON *St Denis*   SP 263303

The saddleback roofed tower on the south side is 14th century. The rest is all of c1863 except for reset 13th century windows in the chancel.

LITTLE PACKINGTON *St Bartholomew*   SP 213843

19th century restoration has left only the Late Norman north and south doorways, some stained glass in the east window, and the Jacobean pulpit.

LONG COMPTON *St Peter & St Paul*   SP 287330

The spacious 13th century nave has a trefoil headed south doorway. The north doorway was reset in the aisle with an arcade of four wide bays of c1300. The tower and chancel are 13th century too, but the former was heightened and given buttresses in the 15th century, and the latter was mostly rebuilt in 1862. The porch and the defaced female effigy within it are 14th century. Of the 15th century are the clerestory and the tiny lean-to roofed chapel beside the chancel, plus some of the stone panels reused in the pulpit.

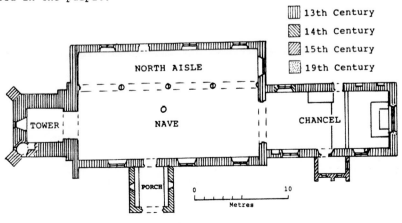

PLAN OF LONG COMPTON CHURCH

41

Long Compton Church

LONG ITCHINGTON *Holy Trinity*

SP 412652

The south doorway with a waterleaf capital on one of the side columns must be of c1190 although the lancets of the aisle look a generation later, and the four bay arcade is 15th century. The nave north side was rebuilt c1300 although the plain mullions in the windows may be 17th century. Of the same period are the two tomb recesses in the aisle and the splendid chancel with sedilia, a double piscina, and Easter Sepulchre of note. It has a 14th century screen. The late 14th century tower has the stump of a spire which fell in 1762. There is a brass inscription with figures of John Bosworth, d1674, and his two wives.

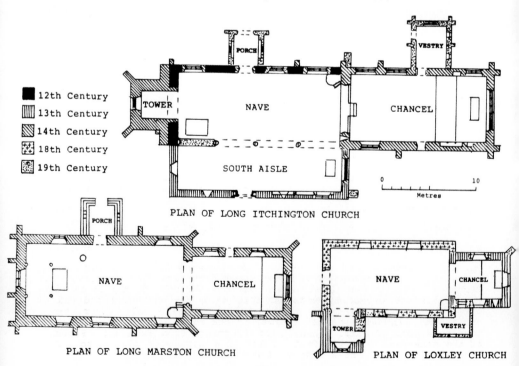

12th Century
13th Century
14th Century
18th Century
19th Century

TOWER NAVE CHANCEL PORCH VESTRY SOUTH AISLE

0 10
Metres

PLAN OF LONG ITCHINGTON CHURCH

PORCH NAVE CHANCEL

PLAN OF LONG MARSTON CHURCH

NAVE CHANCEL TOWER VESTRY

PLAN OF LOXLEY CHURCH

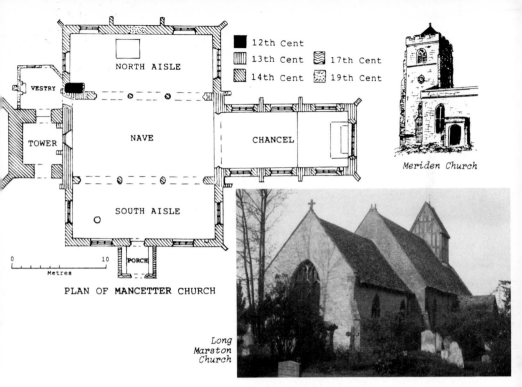

PLAN OF MANCETTER CHURCH

12th Cent
13th Cent
14th Cent
17th Cent
19th Cent

NORTH AISLE

VESTRY

TOWER

NAVE

CHANCEL

SOUTH AISLE

PORCH

0   10
Metres

Meriden Church

Long
Marston
Church

LONG MARSTON *St James*   SP 153482

The nave, chancel, and north porch are all 14th century. The buttresses, except those on the nave east corners, are later, as are the eastern window and the wooden partition walls in the nave west end which carry a timber bell turret, itself Victorian. The pulpit is Jacobean. There is a 17th century bier and the east window has fragments of old glass.

LOWER SHUCKBURGH *St John The Baptist*   SP 499628

A 13th century font lies in the remarkable church of 1864 by Croft.

LOXLEY *St Nicholas*   SP 259531

Much of the church is of the 1730s but the SW tower is 13th century, and the chancel has herringbone masonry internally which may be Norman, while the chancel windows are of c1300. A south aisle has gone. The old furnishings include box pews, a pillar piscina, and a communion rail.

LUDDINGTON *Dedication Unknown*   SP 167525

The font inside the church of 1871-2 lies on the base of an old cross.

MANCETTER *St Peter*   SP 321967

The oldest part is the 13th century nave west wall with a big lancet and clasping buttresses. The tower upper parts are 15th century, but the base, with arches to allow processions through it, may be earlier. The aisles are unusually wide and date from the beginning and end of the 14th century respectively, the south aisle being the later part, and having windows similar to those in the fine chancel, two of which have some good original glass, plus fragments from Merevale. Probably of the same period is the font. There is a strapwork plaque to John Blise, dated 1633, and a bust of Edward Hutton, d1690.

43

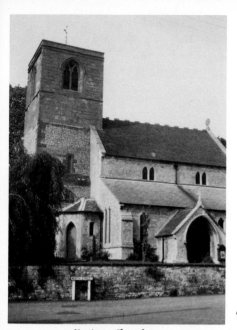

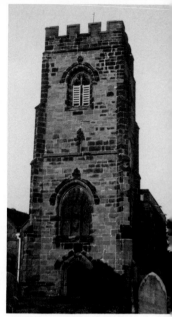

Marton Church   *Brass at Middleton*   *Middleton Church*

MARTON *St Esprit*   SP 407690

The dedication is a very rare one. The south doorway and west tower are
13th century, and the two bay south arcade is 15th century. Most of the
rest including a north aisle, dates from a restoration of 1871.

MAXSTOKE *St Michael*   SP 237868

The church is a wide single chamber built c1340 by William de Clinton.
the coved ceiling, font, pulpit, remains of box pews, the altarpiece
showing St Michael, and the sanctuary panelling, are all 18th century.

MEREVALE *Our Lady*   SP 290977

This church formed the cappella ante portas of a Cistercian Abbey. This
may explain why the chancel is four bays long whilst the nave is only
two. The nave has lost its aisles but retains its 13th century west end.
The chancel and its chapels are of the 14th and 15th centuries. Reset
in the main east window is a 14th century stained glass Tree of Jesse
from the abbey, and three other windows have 14th century glass. A rare
survival is the simple screen lacking both dado and tracery supporting
a loft with a balcony-like projection from its parapet. There are a fine
but damaged military effigy of the late 13th century, brasses of Robert,
Earl Ferrers, d1412, and his wife, and alabaster effigies of a knight
and lady of c1440 with angels against the tomb chest.

MERIDEN *St Lawrence*   SP 252816

The nave east corners and chancel west end with one original window are
Norman, and the chancel east end and the chancel arch are 13th century.
The south arcade looks 14th century but may be as late as 1404 when a
chapel was founded in the aisle. Of later in the 15th century are the
west tower, the three bay north arcade with a stair to the former rood
loft tucked in behind the east respond, and the east window. The aisle
outer walls were rebuilt in the 19th century, and vestries were added
later. There are effigies of knights of c1400 and c1450-60.

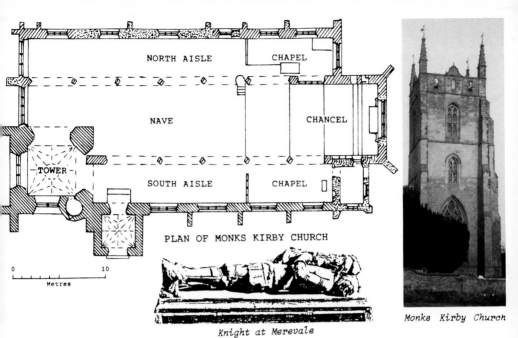

NORTH AISLE   CHAPEL

NAVE   CHANCEL

TOWER

SOUTH AISLE   CHAPEL

PLAN OF MONKS KIRBY CHURCH

0   10

Metres

Knight at Merevale

Monks Kirby Church

MIDDLETON   *St John The Baptist*   SP 177984

The 15th century west tower with crocketted gables over the doorway and windows is said to contain a 14th century bell-frame, a great rarity. The nave is Norman, see the south doorway with chevrons, but there is a 15th century clerestory and much patching. The north aisle and four bay arcade are of c1300. Beyond is an early 19th century vestry. The screen is preserved and there are an 18th century font and a late 17th century pulpit. There are brasses depicting the judge Sir Richard Bingham,d1476, and his wife, a kneeling figure of Thomas Willoughby, Earl of London--derry, d1638, a tablet of Francis Willoughby, d1675, and the busts of Benjamin and Samuel White, d1685 and 1688 respectively.

MONKS KIRBY   *St Edith*   SP 464831

The north side has the windows set high enough to allow for a cloister walk of a Benedictine priory although this side is very restored. The nave seems to have originally been aisleless but a wide south aisle with a fine vaulted porch and a large tower at its west end was added early in the 14th century. In the 15th century the interior was rearranged to give a central nave with two aisles of normal width with arcades up to six bays long. The piers are lozenge shaped and without capitals. A new chancel was built and the 13th century sedilia and piscina reset in it. The tower has a later upper stage which bore a spire until it fell in 1722. In the north aisle is part of a defaced 14th century effigy and in the north chapel are recumbent effigies on tomb chests of two Feildings, Sir William, d1547, and Basil, d1580, with their wives.

MORETON MORRELL   *Holy Cross*   SP 311556

The west tower and the nave and chancel with a row of buttresses along the south side seem mostly 13th century, but the nave may have Norman masonry as a lintel and tympanum lie loose inside and the tower has a reset window perhaps of that date. The north doorway is 15th century. The nave windows and the brick tower top are Georgian. The pulpit has Jacobean panels. There are kneeling figures of Richard Muden, d1635, and his wife facing each other across a prayer desk, and with two putti.

45

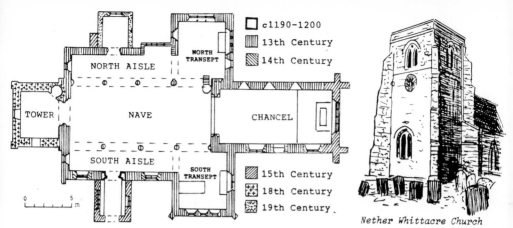

c1190-1200

[III] 13th Century

[\\\] 14th Century

NORTH TRANSEPT

NORTH AISLE

TOWER

NAVE

CHANCEL

SOUTH AISLE

SOUTH TRANSEPT

[///] 15th Century

[+++] 18th Century

[///] 19th Century

0   5
└──────┘ m

Nether Whittacre Church

PLAN OF NAPTON-ON-THE HILL CHURCH

MORTON BAGOT *Holy Trinity*   SP 114647

There is one Norman north window but otherwise the features of the nave
and chancel are mostly of c1300. The end walls and two north buttresses
are perhaps 15th century. The communion rail has panels from an early
16th century screen and there is a rare medieval reading desk.

MOSELEY *St Mary*   SP 078831

This church probably was a chapel-of-ease to King's Norton built in the
15th century. A west tower was added in the early 16th century. It has
brick patching perhaps of 1780 when the church itself was rebuilt. This
was altered in 1823 but was swept away by the successive building of a
new north aisle in 1886, addition of a new chancel and south chapel in
1897, and the rebuilding of the nave and south aisle in 1910. They were
rebuilt again in 1952-4 as a result of bombing damage in 1940.

Morton Bagot Church

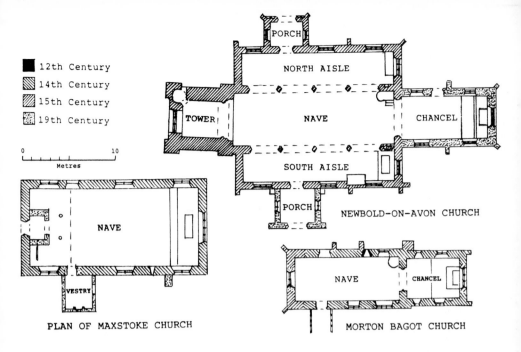

12th Century

14th Century

15th Century

19th Century

0   10
Metres

PORCH

NORTH AISLE

TOWER   NAVE   CHANCEL

SOUTH AISLE

PORCH   NEWBOLD-ON-AVON CHURCH

NAVE

VESTRY

PLAN OF MAXSTOKE CHURCH

NAVE   CHANCEL

MORTON BAGOT CHURCH

NAPTON-ON-THE-HILL *St Laurence*   SP 464613

Most of the church dates from the late 13th century apart from a south doorway of c1200 with stiff-leaf capitals and a roll-moulded round arch. There are aisles with four bay arcades with the eastern bays opening into transepts with triple lancets in their end walls, that on the north having a round arch over. Both transepts have a pair of tomb recesses. The chancel east wall was rebuilt in the 15th century, when a porch was added. Of the 1861 restoration are the chancel south windows and perhaps the arcading made from old parts in the porch. The tower was rebuilt in the 18th century except for the arch of c1300 towards the nave.

NETHER WHITACRE *St Giles*   SP 232928

The ashlar faced west tower is 16th century. The chancel is partly 14th century, and the south window has old glass. The rest is of 1870. There is a large monument by Richard Hayward to Charles Jennens, made c1775.

NEWBOLD-ON-AVON *St Botolph*   SP 486772

The chancel has been rebuilt and a south porch added. Otherwise the red sandstone church is all 15th century. The nave has aisles with four bay arcades, a north porch with rows of canopied niches, and a west tower with big clasping buttresses. The arcade piers have a complex section. The north door with inscriptions in plaques is original, as are some tiles in the south aisle. The communion table is Jacobean. The wrought iron tower screen is early 18th century and once belonged to a monument to Sir William Boughton, d1716, with standing figures of him and his wife. There are kneeling figures of several 16th and early 17th century Boughtons and their wives, and incised slabs on tomb chests to Geoffrey Allesley, d1441, and Thomas Boughton, d1454, and their wives.

NEWBOLD PACEY *St George*   SP 299572

A monument to Edward Carew, d1668, and his infant daughter lies within the church, which was entirely rebuilt in 1881 to a design by Pearson.

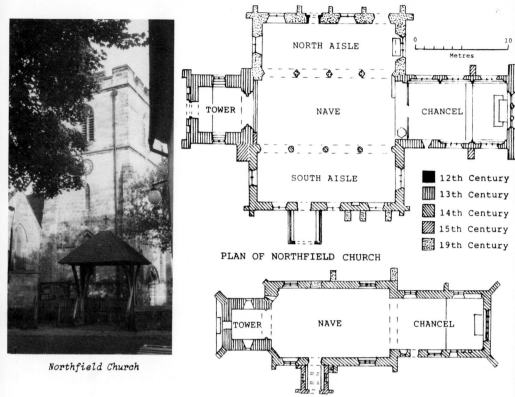

PLAN OF NORTHFIELD CHURCH

■	12th Century
	13th Century
	14th Century
	15th Century
	19th Century

PLAN OF NEWTON REGIS CHURCH

Northfield Church

NEWTON REGIS *St Mary*   SK 279075

The tower is early 13th century but the buttresses and spire are of the 14th century, like the nave and chancel. The NE buttress is pierced by a squint allowing a view of the nave from beside the tower. The chancel has a fine piscina and an Easter Sepulchre. The rib vaulted porch may date from c1400 like similar ones in Nottinghamshire. The clerestory and battlements of the nave are 15th century. An early 14th century coffin lid has ballflowers on the rim and The Lamb carrying a cross in the head of which is the bust of a priest. The pulpit and tester are of the 18th century. The painted pattern on the north windows may be old.

NORTHFIELD *St Lawrence*   SP 026794

The north aisle dates from 1900 and the vestries beyond it are of 1959. Otherwise this is a fine medieval church still in a village setting in spite of now being part of Birmingham. The oldest parts are the reset Norman doorway in the north aisle, and two windows with carved animal heads on the tower. The tower is otherwise late 13th century with a 15th century top stage. The splendid 13th century chancel has triple lancet groups to the east, north, and south, plus a low side window on the south. Instead of a chancel arch there are four adjacent trusses of the roof, an arrangement apparently contemporary with the 15th century chancel roof. Above it, facing the nave, there was probably a painting of the Last Judgement. The wide south aisle with a four bay arcade on octagonal piers is early 14th century. It seems to have replaced a narrow earlier aisle. The timber south porch is 15th century, as are the fragments of the former screen now reused in the pulpit.

NORTON LINDSEY *Holy Trinity*   SP 230631

This is a tiny 13th century church of nave and chancel with a 14th century east window in the latter. The north aisle, vestry, and south windows are of 1874. The pulpit has panels of 1682 and the early 17th century.

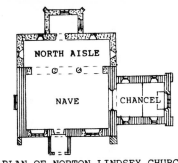

PLAN OF NORTON LINDSEY CHURCH

NUNEATON *St Mary*   SP 366916

Of an aisleless cruciform Benedictine nuns' church founded in the 1150s there survive the massive piers of the central tower. The chancel and north transept were rebuilt in 1236-8 after the original tower fell, and again in 1906 and 1930. The eastern part of the nave was rebuilt in the 19th century but the western part and the south transept remain ruined. The north transept seems to have served a parish and once had a porch.

NUNEATON *St Nicholas*   SP 363912

The church is isolated from the town centre by a ring road. Of the 14th century are the north aisle, north chapel, and south chapel with its three bay arcade, piscina combined with a credence shelf, and sedilia with ogee heads. The two bay north chapel arcade and nave arcades are later. The wall above the latter is panelled up to a clerestory. The west tower and the stair turret on the south side which provided access to a rood loft are 15th century. In 1852 the south aisle and chancel were rebuilt. The 18th century galleries were removed in 1965. There is a recumbent effigy of Sir Marmaduke Constable d1560, and a bust of Anthony Trotman, d1703.

St Nicholas' Church, Nuneaton

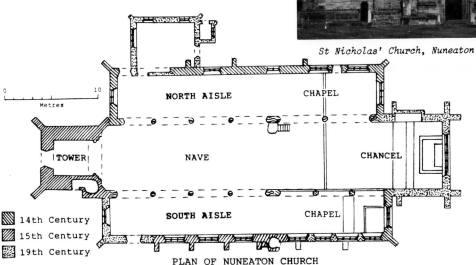

PLAN OF NUNEATON CHURCH

Oldberrow
Church

Polesworth Church

OFFCHURCH *St Gregory*   SP 358657

Both nave and chancel are Norman with some original windows and a north
doorway with one order of columns. The chancel was remodelled and made
longer in the late 13th century. The south doorway and reset outer arch
of the porch are 13th century although the porch itself is 14th or 15th
century. The west tower is 15th century. The pulpit is 18th century.

OLDBERROW *St Mary*   SP 122660

The church was rebuilt in 1875 but retains a Norman window, south and
north doorways of the 14th and 15th centuries respectively, a lancet of
c1200, and east and SE windows of c1300, plus an old font.

OVER WHITACRE *St Leonard*   SP 255910

The church bears the date 1766 and may have been designed by William or
David Hiorn. It consists of a west tower bearing a spire of 1850 instead
of the original dome, a three bay nave with arched windows and a short
chancel with a Venetian east window.

OXHILL *St Laurence*   SP 316455

The Norman chancel north windows have chevron hood-moulds. The nave has
a similar window and two doorways each with two orders of shafts. There
are chevrons on the south doorway. The font with intersecting arches,
Adam and Eve, and other motifs, and the chancel arch are Norman too, but
the latter has been altered. The chancel south windows, the nave south
buttresses, west tower, and clerestory are 15th century, the porch is
14th century, and the east wall is a 19th century rebuild. There are
old bench ends and the tower screen incorporated old material.

PACKWOOD *St Giles*   SP 170728

The nave and chancel are mostly of c1300. A west tower was added in the
early 16th century, and in 1704 a transeptal family chapel of brick was
added on the north. The chapel was subsequently gothicised. There is a
late medieval screen. One bench end is old. There are paintings of the
Three Quick and the Three Dead either side of the chancel arch although
the latter are very faint. One window contains a 14th century crucifixion
and there are other fragments of old glass. There are numerous tablets
the best being that to John Fetherston, d1670.

50

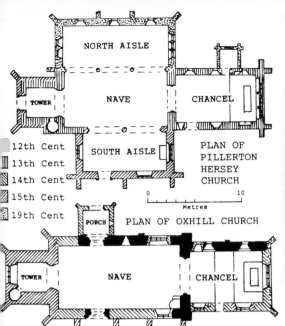

NORTH AISLE

TOWER

NAVE

CHANCEL

PLAN OF
PILLERTON
HERSEY
CHURCH

SOUTH AISLE

■ 12th Cent
▥ 13th Cent
▨ 14th Cent
▧ 15th Cent
▦ 19th Cent

0   10
Metres

PLAN OF OXHILL CHURCH

PORCH

TOWER

NAVE

CHANCEL

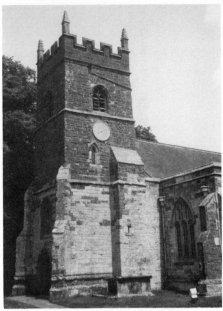

Pillerton Hersey Church

PILLERTON HERSEY *St Mary*   SP 298488

The splendid mid 13th century chancel has single lancets on each side, a triple east lancet under a shafted arch with a cusped quatrefoil in a circle, a fine moulded priest's doorway, and double piscina and aumbry. The tower seems 13th century too, but remodelled in the 15th century. The south aisle with a two bay arcade is of c1400 but is restored while the north aisle is all of 1845. The nave has a low pitched 15th century roof with bosses. The chancel has a hammerbeam roof of the 17th century.

POLESWORTH *St Edith*   SK 264024

The church served a Benedictine nunnery which had a cloister against the south side, which explains why the windows there are set high up. The building comprises a nave and aisle of equal width, a chancel, and set against the latter a mighty 14th century NE tower with a later top. The exterior is otherwise mostly renewed and so is much of the eight bay arcade, but the two east arches are of c1120-30. Below them is an effigy of an abbess of c1200. On a tomb chest is a 15th century female effigy of alabaster on a tomb chest. There is also a 14th century Crucifixion.

PRESTON BAGOT *All Saints*   SP 175661

The nave has two doorways and several windows which are Norman. The Late Norman chancel was remodelled c1300 and the east wall rebuilt in 1879. The nave also has some 14th and 19th century windows.

PRESTON-ON-STOUR *St Mary*   SP 204499

The west tower and low pitched nave roof with bosses are 15th century. The nave south wall may be earlier but the windows match the new north wall and chancel with a panelled ceiling of 1752-64 designed by Edward Woodward of Chipping Campden. The font, screen, stalls, and gallery all go with the remodelling but some of the glass is 16th and 17th century. There are kneeling effigies of Sir Nicholas Kemp, d1624, with two wives set either side of him, a monument to Thomas Steavons, d1759, and some later monuments to members of the West family of Alscot Park.

Ratley Church

PRIORS HARDWICK *St Mary* SP 473563

The lower part of the short and small west tower, the nave masonry and the chancel with several windows with different types of Geometrical tracery and splendid sedilia and piscina are all late 13th century. The nave was mostly rebuilt in 1868 and a vestry added on the north side. There are fragments of an incised slab of a 15th century knight.

PRIORS MARSTON *St Leonard* SP 489577

The five bay north arcade and aisle walling may be 13th century although there are early 16th century windows with uncusped lights. The chancel was rebuilt in the 1860s and the south windows of the nave renewed, but the south doorway is 15th century. The early 18th century tower has Y-tracery in rounded headed windows and clasping pilaster buttresses.

QUINTON *St Swithun* SP 184470

The eastern two bays of the south arcade are mid 12th century. At the end of the century the western bay was added and the north arcade of four pointed arches was built. The aisle walls were rebuilt in the early 14th century when the west tower was begun and the chancel arch renewed. The chancel itself is 13th century, although the east window is Victorian. The tower top and spire and clerestory are 15th century. The Norman font has scallops underneath. Over the chancel arch are the arms of Elizabeth I. The church acquired the 14th century sculpture of the Virgin, and the female saint of c1500 only c1930. In the north chapel is some old glass. On a tomb chest is a brass of c1430 to Lady Clopton, and there is also a tablet with putti to Thomas Lingen, d1742.

RADFORD SEMELE *St Nicholas* SP 343638

The north aisle, vestry, and chancel are all of 1889, but the west tower is 15th century and the nave has a Norman south wall with one window.

RADWAY *St Peter* SP 368481

The church was rebuilt in 1866. One old window head is reset in a shed. The Dutch 17th century glass in a chancel window was in Edgehill Tower.

RATLEY *St Peter Ad Vincula* SP 384473

The chancel is of c1300, and the nave and aisle with a three bay arcade are of c1340. Slightly later are the south chapel and west tower, and the porch may be 15th century. The windows are generally unrestored. The shaft and part of the head with a Crucifixion remain of a churchyard cross to the south of the church.

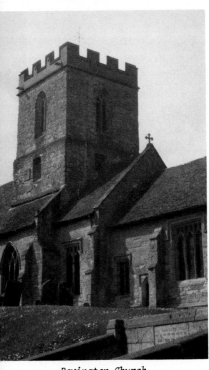

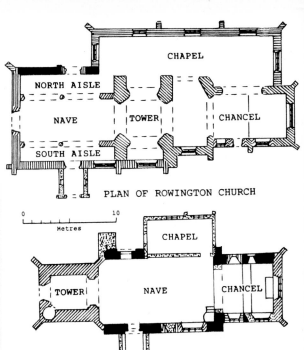

PLAN OF ROWINGTON CHURCH

0   10
       Metres

PLAN OF RYTON-ON-DUNSMORE CHURCH

Rowington Church

ROWINGTON *St Lawrence*   SP 205694

The church has a peculiar plan and is a hotchpotch of different periods. The nave north wall with a pilaster buttress is Norman. In the 1280s the nave was given a new west wall and considerably widened southwards. Then in c1300 was built a tower on four arches within this nave and the bay to the east which may represent the width of the intended chancel. In the event when a chancel was built shortly after it was made narrower. In c1490 this chancel was given new south windows and the nave gained a pair of two bay arcades creating narrow aisles. The west doorway and the ceiled wagon roof with bosses are of about the same time. A long north chapel was added in 1552. It retains its original screen. The communion rail dates from 1682. There is a rare 15th century stone pulpit. There are also fragments of old glass, and a tablet to John Wollaston, d1615.

RUGBY *St Andrew*   SP 504752

The rebuilding and enlargement by Butterfield in 1877-85 has left little of the medieval church. The original nave has become a wide north aisle and has a plain unbuttressed 14th century tower west of it. The original north aisle, now an outer aisle, is medieval in origin but is all rebuilt. The only old furnishing is a 13th century chest with iron scrolls.

RYTON-ON-DUNSMORE *St Leonard*   SP 386745

Both nave and chancel have walling of c1080-1100 with several original windows and two nave doorways. Other windows are of an assortment of periods; 13th, 15th, and 16th century, plus lunettes of c1800 when the porch was added. The north chapel is of 1812 and the west tower is 15th century. The pulpit is Jacobean. The communion rail is late 17th century. Two traceried panels on the stalls have probably come from the screen.

53

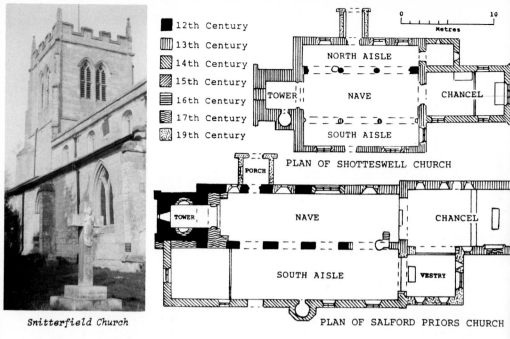

■	12th Century
⦀	13th Century
⧄	14th Century
⧅	15th Century
☰	16th Century
▨	17th Century
⋰	19th Century

PLAN OF SHOTTESWELL CHURCH

PLAN OF SALFORD PRIORS CHURCH

Snitterfield Church

SALFORD PRIORS *St Matthew*   SP 077510

The Norman west tower with clasping buttresses bears the date 1633. That
may be when it was made larger and given new bell openings. Late in the
12th century a south aisle was made by piercing three pointed arches
through the nave wall leaving sections of wall between them. The fourth
bay was made in the 13th century when a new chancel, wider than the old
nave, was built further east. The aisle was doubled in width and given
a polygonal stair turret in the 14th century. The chancel lancets have
rere-arches, as have two more in the nave north wall either side of a
large 14th century window. In the aisle are panels with monsters and a
hunting scene, reused at one time in a pulpit. There is a large tablet
of 1631 to Dame Margaret Clarke and her sons Walter and Thomas. Other
Clarke monuments are those of Margaret, d1640, and Dorothy, d1669.

SECKINGTON *All Saints*   SK 259075

The heavily restored nave, chancel, and south porch are all of the early
14th century, the period of the defaced female effigy in the blocked
north doorway. The doorways and double piscina are ogee headed. There
are fragments of contemporary glass and tracery from the dado of the
screen. The west tower is earlier, say 1270 to 1300, and has diagonal
buttresses with chamfered ends, and a 15th century parapet and spire.
Kneeling effigies of Robert Burdett, d1603, and his wife and family
face each other across a prayer desk. They are carved from alabaster.

SHELDON *St Giles*   SP 153846

This pretty church lies on the eastern boundary of Birmingham. It has a
nave of 1330 with a fine contemporary roof of four trusses with curved
braces to the cambered tie-beams. A north aisle with a three bay arcade
was added c1360, but except for the arcade and north doorway was rebuilt
in 1887, as was the chancel. The west tower bears an inscription on the
south side dating it to 1461. The nave was extended westwards to join up
with it. The timber framed south porch is early 16th century. The font
and the reredos now in the aisle are 15th century.

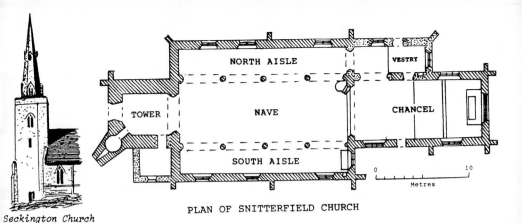

Seckington Church

PLAN OF SNITTERFIELD CHURCH

SHILTON *St Andrew*   SP 404844

The 13th century chancel retains two lancets. The nave and north aisle
are 14th century. The fourth bay of the aisle has a separate arch and it
seems a NW tower was intended, but an ordinary west tower was built in
the 15th century, and the timber south porch also added. Parts of the
screen survive and some fragments of old glass in the west window.

SHIPSTON-ON-STOUR *St Edmund*   SP 260406

Only the 15th century west tower and the bust of John Hart, d1747, plus
the sounding board of a pulpit made into a table survived the rebuilding
of the church by Street in 1855.

SHOTTESWELL *St Lawrence*   SP 427455

The nave, three bay arcades, west tower, and chancel arch are all 13th
century, although the north arcade is Norman and the windows are later,
15th century on the south, 19th century on the north where there is a
Victorian porch. The chancel and the vestry with an ogee headed doorway
to the north aisle are later 14th century and of about the same period
is the screen with cusped semicircles and shafts rather than the later
mullions. Panels with late medieval tracery are reused in the stalls,
pulpit, benches, and tower screen. The communion rail is 17th century.

SHUSTOKE *St Cuthbert*   SP 243910

This is a wide naved red sandstone church mostly of c1320-50. The nave
windows have ballflowers as hood mould stops. The chancel has a pretty
double piscina. Relics of a Norman church are one window reset in the
north vestry and a capital and a stone with dogtooth ornament lying in
the porch. There is a tomb chest of Sir William Dugdale, d1685.

SHUTTINGTON *St Matthew*   SK 255052

The nave has a west doorway with one order of columns and chevrons plus
traces of Norman north and south doorways. The windows are Victorian.
There are a weatherboarded bellcote and an 18th century pulpit.

SNITTERFIELD *St James*   SP 218601

Much of the church, which has a spacious heavily restored chancel, and
four bay arcades, plus many windows with Y-tracery, is of c1300, and the
west tower is only slightly later. It has a huge SW buttress containing
a stair. Also 14th century is the font with heads coming out from under
it. The south arcade arches with their peculiar capitals are probably
15th century like the clerestory. There are stall fronts and ends of
the 1530s, a Jacobean communion rail, and an 18th century pulpit.

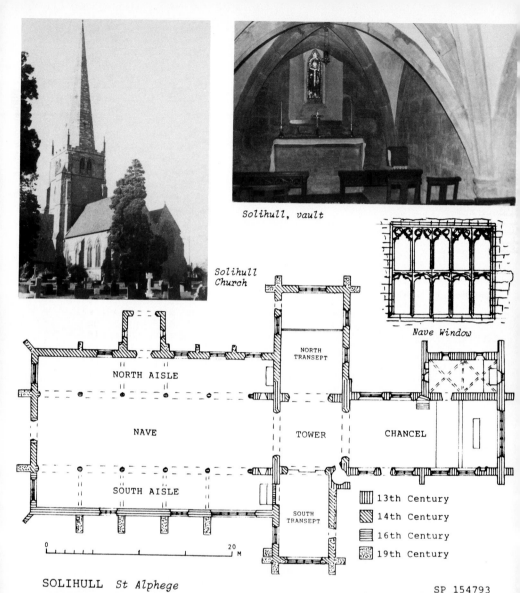

Solihull, vault

Solihull Church

Nave Window

NORTH TRANSEPT

NORTH AISLE

NAVE

TOWER

CHANCEL

SOUTH AISLE

SOUTH TRANSEPT

0   20
         M

||||| 13th Century

\\\\\ 14th Century

≡≡≡ 16th Century

⋮⋮⋮ 19th Century

SOLIHULL *St Alphege*   SP 154793

The arches below the crossing tower of this large red sandstone church
are 13th century although the tower itself and recessed spire are 15th
century. Immediately west of the tower, before the leaning arcades of
five bays begin, are short blank sections of walling with traces of 12th
century windows, showing the nave was then unaisled. The present north
aisle wall and north porch are of c1330. The nave and aisles otherwise
were rebuilt in the 1530s. There are Victorian flying buttresses inside
with heavy supports outside on the south. The transepts are of c1300 and
of unequal size, that on the north being longer and wider. The splendid
chancel and the chapel of St Alphege above a vaulted undercroft on the
north side with a steeply pitched separate roof are of c1290-1310. There
are brasses to William Gill, d1549, and William Hawes, d1610, and their
wives, and two incised slabs.

Brass at Solihull

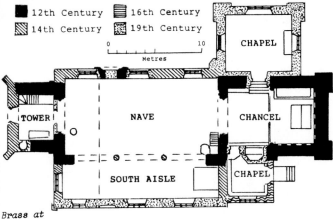

PLAN OF STONELEIGH CHURCH

SOUTHAM *St James*   SP 417617

The north side is all Victorian and the rest is much restored, except for the 14th century arcades, the south aisle tomb recesses, the fine 15th century clerestory, and the 14th century west tower with a slightly later broach spire. The church is built of red sandstone. The pulpit is probably Jacobean, though with late medieval type tracery panels.

SPERNALL *St Leonard*   SP 086622

The nave has two 14th century windows but the west window is slightly earlier and the north doorway later. The door in it has panels of c1535. One window has some old glass. The chancel was rebuilt in 1844.

STOCKTON *St Michael*   SP 437637

The nave and aisles are entirely of 1863-73 but the chancel has some 14th century features, and the tower is 15th century.

STOKE *St Michael*   SP 331768

Most of this church in Coventry suburbia dates from 1861, but the west tower, with some original glass, and the font are 15th century, three western bays of the south aisle are of c1320-30, the piscina is a late 13th century capital with a head, and there is an 18th century tablet.

STONELEIGH *St Mary*   SP 331726

The tower, nave, and chancel are all Norman work of some ambition. The tower has a blocked north window and a 15th century upper part. The arch to the nave has many scallop capitals. The north doorway of two orders with scallops, bobbins, and pellets on the hoodmould, has a tympanum with interlocked necked dragons biting their own tails, as do two snakes on a panel above. The chancel arch is particularly fine and has chevrons not only on the arch but on the responds as well. The chancel was meant to be vaulted in two bays and has restored internal arcading. The font with the twelve apostles in arcading is Norman too, but originally lay in Maxstoke church. The nave has north windows of c1300 with intersecting tracery and a 14th century south aisle. On either side of the chancel are a vaulted south chapel of 1665, and large early 19th century north chapel with a tierceron star-vault of plaster. Many of the furnishings are early 19th century and three notable monuments are Victorian. Earlier are the 18th century communion rail, a defaced 14th century effigy, an effigy of a 15th century priest, and a large black and white marble tomb with effigies of Alice, Duchess Dudley, d1668, and her daughter.

Stratford-On-Avon Church

STRATFORD-ON-AVON *Holy Trinity* SP 201544

This church is a large cruciform structure lying by the river away from the town centre. The transepts and lower parts of the central tower are 13th century, and small blocked arches indicate that at that time both the chancel and nave had narrow aisles. The crossing arches were rebuilt in the 14th century when the long present nave and aisles with arcades of six bays were laid out on a different axis to the rest of the church. The south aisle roof with bosses and the rose windows in the tower are of that period, during which a college was founded by John de Stratford, later made Bishop of Winchester.

The chancel was rebuilt by Dean Balshall, d1491, whose tomb, which once had a brass upon it, lies on the north side. The chancel is a fine structure of five bays with large four light side windows, a seven light east window, and decorated buttresses and panelled parapets. A two storey sacristy on the north side has been removed. Other monuments within the chancel include a bust of William Shakespeare, d1616, effigies of Judith Comb, d1649, and her betrothed, and a bust of James Kendall, d1756, who is depicted in Roman costume.

Dean Balshall's successor Collingwood, d1521, probably erected the north porch and the twelve bay clerestory with blank panelling reaching down to the arcade arches, and also the nine light west window. At the east end of the north aisle is the Clopton chapel containing the tomb chest of Hugh Clopton, d1496, alabaster effigies of William Clopton, d1592, and his wife, and effigies of Joyce Clopton and her spouse George Carew, Earl of Totnes and Lord Clopton, d1629.

Of old furnishings there are a disused font bowl, a screen closing off the north transept, parts of the main screen, choir stalls with a fine series of carved miserichords of c1500 with many scenes and motifs of interest, the main north door and the tower door, fragments of old stained glass, and an 18th century sword rest.

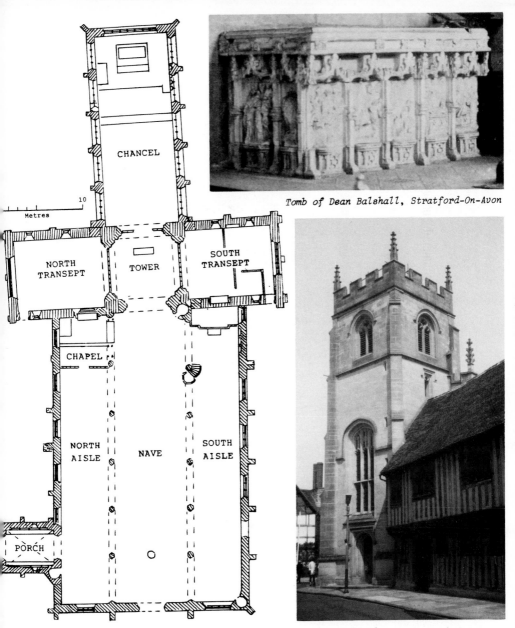

CHANCEL

NORTH TRANSEPT

TOWER

SOUTH TRANSEPT

CHAPEL

NORTH AISLE

NAVE

SOUTH AISLE

PORCH

10

Metres

Tomb of Dean Balshall, Stratford-On-Avon

PLAN OF STRATFORD-ON-AVON CHURCH

Guild Chapel at Stratford-On-Avon

STRATFORD-ON-AVON   *Guild Chapel of Holy Cross*   SP 201547

The chancel of c1430-50 seems modest compared with the new four bay nave
with a west tower and north porch built by Sir Hugh Clopton in the late
15th century. There are large four light windows and battlements. Over
the chancel arch is a Doom painting and there are relics of other wall
paintings at the west end. The marble font is 18th century.

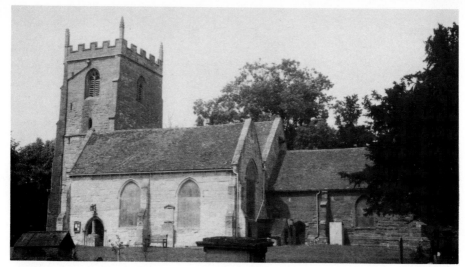

Studley Church

STUDLEY *Nativity of The Virgin* SP 082638

The Norman nave north wall has herringbone masonry, a doorway with one order of shafts with a later doorway set within it and a small window high up. The other windows go with the south aisle of c1320-30 with a three bay arcade. The chancel is perhaps late 14th century and contains a large 13th century coffin lid with a foliated cross and a lengthy inscription referring to one of the priors of the nearby priory. The west tower is 15th century. The sculptured panel with a Lamb and Cross may be Norman. There is an 18th century baluster font with a fluted bowl, and the communion rail and pulpit are 17th century.

SUTTON COLDFIELD *Holy Trinity* SP 122963

This church lies on an eminence forming an open space between the main streets of the old and new centres of the town. Remaining from the early medieval period are the Norman font carved with intersecting arches and heads with sprigs of foliage coming out of the mouths, and the shallow buttresses of the chancel east wall. The west tower is 14th century and the south aisle is 16th century. Bishop Veysey of Exeter, d1554, has his effigy on a tomb chest in the north chapel, and an inscription on the tomb suggests he built both the chancel chapels. The round arched nave arcades with three wider bays and two narrower western bays are probably of after 1759, when part of the nave collapsed and was rebuilt at the expense of the corporation. The outer north aisle is a blatant Victorian addition of 1875-9 and there are 20th century vestries.

The interior has much of interest apart from the Veysey tomb and the font. There are monuments to Henry Pudsey, d1677, and Henry Jesson, d1705. The fine pulpit and tester are of c1740-50, the dado of the main screen is Jacobean, and the north chapel screen is said to be made of parts of a mid 17th century organ case and stalls from Worcester Cathedral. The south chapel and tower screens also have 17th century work, and there is an 18th century south gallery.

SUTTON-UNDER-BRAILES *St Thomas Beckett* SP 299374

The nave is Norman, see the north doorway. The chancel is 13th century. New windows were inserted in the east end and in the nave in c1300. The early 14th century porch-tower on the south is the only ashlar faced part. The recess on the north side is probably 16th century. The west wall was rebuilt in the 19th century.

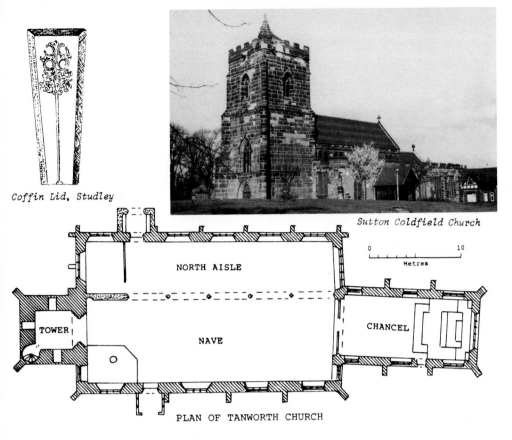

Coffin Lid, Studley

Sutton Coldfield Church

PLAN OF TANWORTH CHURCH

TANWORTH-IN-ARDEN *St Mary Magdalene* SP 114705

The west tower, nave, north aisle, and chancel are all work of c1300-25 on a generous scale. The setting out is odd with the arches to the tower and chancel being in line with each other but far out from the central axis of the nave. The five light east window has cusped intersecting tracery with pointed trefoils. The tower has a spire recessed behind a plain parapet. A wall replaced the arcade in 1790, but in 1880 a new set of arches were built, a porch added, and the aisle window tracery renewed. The church has a few medieval tiles below the image platforms by the east wall, a large 13th century chest, and a baluster shaped 18th century font. Of an early 16th century brass of a family only the small figures of the children survive. The large monument to Thomas Archer, d1685, and his wife was probably designed by their son Thomas.

TEMPLE BALSALL *St Mary* SP 207760

This large four bay single chamber about 31m by 11m externally was once the chapel of a Templar preceptory. It dates from c1280 but was altered in c1680 to serve a hospital built alongside, and was mostly rebuilt in 1849. There was originally a vaulted porch at the SW corner.

TIDMINGTON *Dedication unknown* SP 262386

There are Norman north and south doorways. Otherwise the nave is mostly of 1874. The tower with clasping corner pilasters and chancel arch are 13th century. The chancel has 15th century windows. One bench end is old.

Tredington Church

TREDINGTON *St Gregory*   SP 259436

Above the three bay arcades of c1160 there survives masonry of a nave of c1100. The evidence of blocked windows suggests it had a gallery at the west end. The south doorway is of c1200. The west tower, aisles, and chancel are all early 14th century. Several windows have reticulated tracery. The spire recessed behind an openwork parapet, the clerestory, and two storey north porch, the benches, and the screen set upon a stone base are all 15th century. The fine pulpit is Jacobean. The lectern may be late medieval. A late 17th century communion rail now lies under the tower arch. On the chancel floor are brasses to a 15th century priest and Henry Sampson, d1482.

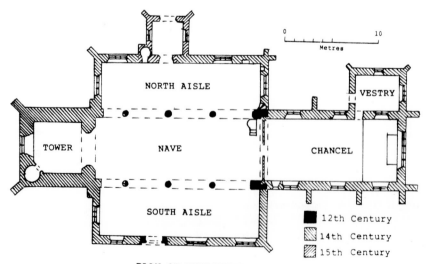

PLAN OF TREDINGTON CHURCH

62

TYSOE *Assumption*
SP 342443

The south arcade was originally of three bays built c1150 but was given new pointed arches after a fourth west bay was built to connect up with the tower of c1200. Older Norman windows survive above the arcade. Late in the 13th century the tower was given a new arch, and the bell stage was added in the 15th century. The aisle south wall was rebuilt c1330-40 and given a porch but the inner doorway is a good piece of c1190 with two orders of columns with shaft rings and waterleaf capitals, a chain of lozenges in the arch, and a panel with the Lamb and Cross above. The north aisle is 14th century, the chancel is late 15th century, and the north chapel is Victorian, but with a reset 14th century window. On the 15th century font are saints and the Virgin under crocketted gables. A few benches have poppy heads, others are Jacobean. A recess in the north aisle has a coffin lid with a cross and the head and shoes of a man. A recess in the chancel contains the effigy of William Clarke, d1618. There are brasses to Thomas Mastrupe, d1463, and Jane Gibbs, d1598.

UFTON *St Michael*
SP 378622

The chancel of c1300 has two low-side lancets near the west end. Earlier are the south doorway with nailhead decoration and the three bay south arcade. The 14th century north aisle probably had four bays but is now reduced to two. Alternatively, the two west bays remained unbuilt. The west tower is 15th century. There are benches with lions' heads, some fragments of the screen made into a reading desk, and a Jacobean pulpit. The churchyard cross has a Crucifixion, St Mary, St Chad, & St Catherine.

ULLENHALL *St Mary*
SP 122673

A new church 2km to the SW was built in 1875 and of the old church only the chancel with features of c1300 now remains. It contains some 17th century panelling, a wrought iron communion rail dated 1635, and the monument with columns and putti to Francis Throckmorton, d1617.

UPPER SHUCKBURGH *St John The Baptist*
SP 497618

Except for parts of the tower and some late 16th century heraldic glass the church and its furnishings are Victorian but there are many notable monuments to the Shuckburgh family. In the south chapel are recumbent effigies of John, d1691, and his wife, and a bust of Richard, d1651. In the north chapel are brasses to a lady of c1500 and Thomas, d1549, and his wife, plus a marble monument to Sir Stukeley, d1759. In the chancel are brasses of Anthony, d1594, and his wife, a large tablet and bust of Catherine, d1683, and a tablet with crying putti to John, d1724. There are many more of later date in the nave.

WALSGRAVE-ON-SOWE *St Mary*
SP 379809

The Norman flower pot shaped font with arcading is the earliest feature. The sandstone chancel with Y-tracery in the windows is of c1300, the nave and aisles are 14th and 15th century, and the west tower is 15th century. A large porch and vestry complex has recently been built to the south.

WALTON *St James*
SP 285525

Near the hall is a chapel of 1750. The recessed Tuscan west porch and bellcote, plus the ceiling, are modifications of 1842.

WAPPENBURY *St John The Baptist*
SP 378693

The 13th century chancel has three lancets on each side, a triple east lancet group under one hoodmould, and trefoil headed priest's doorway and piscina. The nave and south aisle were mostly rebuilt in 1886 when a porch was added, but the SW tower is 15th century. One upper window is a reset 13th century lancet.

Beauchamp
Chapel
Warwick

WARMINGTON *St Michael*

SP 411475

Both arcades are Late Norman and were originally of three bays having pointed arches. Probably the more substantial north piers were erected first. The south aisle was enlarged in the late 13th century, having a good east window of that period, and the north aisle was enlarged when the chancel was rebuilt and the arcades given a fourth arch in the 14th century. North of the chancel is a vestry with barred windows and a room for a priest above. A window from the latter looks down on the altar. This structure is as massive as, and bigger than, the late 14th century west tower. There are old doors in the vestry and part of the screen.

WARWICK *St Mary*

SP 283650

The church was made collegiate in 1123. Under patronage of successive Earls of Warwick it was rebuilt on a large scale. Of the Norman church the only relic is the large rib vaulted crypt with sturdy round pillars with scalloped capitals. In the 1360s the crypt was extended to support a spacious new chancel completed in 1392. This chancel has four bays of tierceron vaulting, a huge six light east window with panel tracery, and much blank panelling on the inner wall faces. In the centre is the tomb of Thomas Beauchamp, d1369, who sponsored the rebuilding. On the north are contemporary vestries with a polygonal ended chapter house beyond. In them are some old glass and monuments to Fulke Greville, d1626, Sir Thomas Puckering, d1639, and Francis Parker, d1693. On the south side is a chapel created from an earlier two storied vestry. It has an old door near which is an arch intended for a tomb chest.

Richard Beauchamp, d1439, had the splendid Beauchamp Chapel built under the terms of his will. It has a lierne vault with bosses depicting subjects like God The Father and The Assumption, blank panelling on the inside and outside wall faces, a huge seven light east window set above a low vestry, and on the south a series of six-light windows with flying buttresses between them. Among the internal mouldings of the east window are high quality statues of angels and saints. There are two tiers of image canopies in the east corners. The portal giving into the chapel from the south transept matches it exactly but is of 1704. In the middle of the chapel is Richard's tomb chest with a copper gilt bronze effigy. Other monuments include those of 3 year old Robert Dudley, Lord Denbigh, d1584, Robert Dudley, Earl of Leicester, d1588, Ambrose Dudley, Earl of Warwick, d1590, the Countess of Leicester, d1634, and Lady Katherine Leveson, d1678. On the west wall is a partial copy of Michaelangelo's Last Judgement painted by Richard Bird in 1678. There is some original glass in the east window. The reredos is of c1775. The stalls of c1450 are remarkably plain compared with the rest of the chapel.

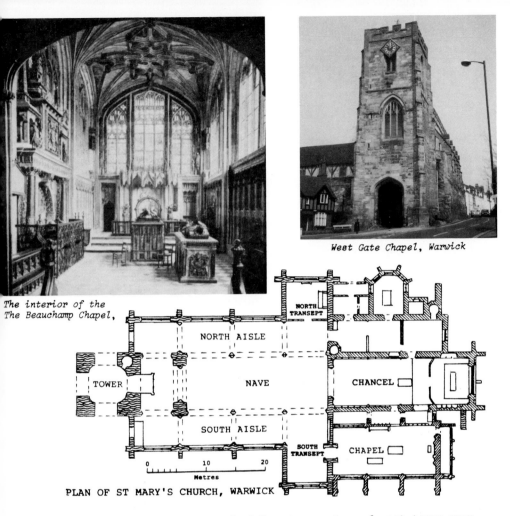

The interior of the
The Beauchamp Chapel,

West Gate Chapel, Warwick

PLAN OF ST MARY'S CHURCH, WARWICK

In 1694 the medieval nave and aisles, transepts, and west tower were gutted by a fire that destroyed much of the town. Wren was paid £12 for making a design for rebuilding but when the work was finally executed by the Smith brothers in 1678-1704 it was to a curious semi-gothic design by Sir William Wilson. The shapes are bald and plain and classical ideas such as balustrades and urns appear. The old layout was kept, although enlarged slightly, but the aisles were now made as high as the nave to create a hall-church, and both are covered by ribbed vaults of plaster. The western piers of the arcades are much larger than the others. They were for a tower which was dismantled after being taken one stage above the main roof because it showed signs of settlement. The present tower, immediately to the west, acts as a porch and has high round arches to the north, west, and south. It is 52m high and has an openwork top with eight pinnacles, those at the corners being higher than the intermediates. The transepts have pediments, a classical rather than gothic treatment.

In the south transept are fine brasses of Thomas Beauchamp, d1401, and his wife, and monuments to Henry Beaufoy and his wife, c1700, Thomas Hewett, d1737, and William Hiorn, d1776. The nave and aisles contain an organ case partly of 1730, a wrought iron screen, once higher, and an 18th century font.

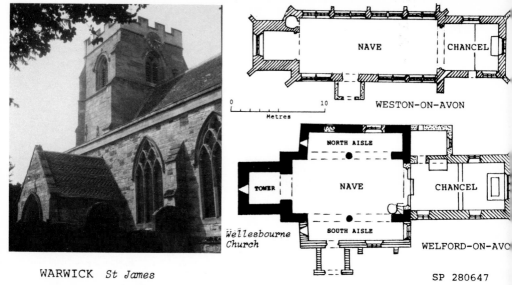

NAVE   CHANCEL

WESTON-ON-AVON

0   10

Metres

NORTH AISLE

TOWER   NAVE   CHANCEL

SOUTH AISLE

Wellesbourne
Church   WELFORD-ON-AVO

WARWICK *St James*   SP 280647

This chapel now forms part of Leycester's Hospital. It lies above the
West Gate of the town walls and the long passageway was extended still
further in the 15th century to support the west tower then added. The
chapel of St Peter above the East Gate was rebuilt in 1788.

WARWICK *St Nicholas*   SP 287650

A tower of 1748 was refaced when the church was rebuilt in 1779-80. The
chancel was added in 1869-70. There is a brass to Robert Willardsey, a
vicar, d1425, and a tablet to Katherine Stoughton, d1724.

WEDDINGTON *St James*   SP 360936

The brick tower, nave, and chancel are of 1881 but there is a medieval
north transept (now a vestry) containing a monument of c1640 to two men
both called Humphrey Adderley. The Norman font has intersecting arches.

WELFORD-ON-AVON *St Peter*   SP 146523

The two bay arcades with scalloped capitals on short piers, the north
aisle with a doorway and west window, and the west tower, are all Norman.
One north window is 15th century. The 14th century chancel was restored
in the 1860s. The south aisle bears the dates 1568 and 1673 and has a
straight headed south window with hood mould stops of a king and queen.
The tower top is 13th century. There is some old glass in the chancel.
The pulpit is Jacobean. The font supports are late 16th century.

WELLESBOURNE *St Peter*   SP 277556

The west tower is 15th century. The remainder was mostly rebuilt in 1847
except for the 13th century five bay south arcade, the impressive chancel
arch of c1100 now reset to open into the organ chamber, and perhaps the
late 14th century looking SW window. A brass of Sir Thomas le Straunge,
d1426, in armour, lies on the floor.

WESTON-ON-AVON *All Saints*   SP 159520

The whole church is of c1480-1500. It comprises an embattled nave with
large six-light windows, a west tower, and chancel. Of a south chapel a
squint into the chancel and the two bay arcade to the nave survive. By
the pulpit are medieval tiles. The bier and wall panelling are of the
17th century. There are brasses to Sir John and Sir Edward Grevill, the
former, d1546, being far better than the latter, d1559.

WESTON-UNDER-WETHERLEY *St Michael* SP 361693

The chancel has some Norman masonry with the jambs of two windows, but the priest's doorway is the same age as the comparatively unaltered north aisle with a three bay arcade. Both aisle and chancel have east windows with intersecting tracery of c1300. The former now looks into a 15th century north chapel. The nave south windows are of c1300, the font is a little later, whilst the tower may be closer to 1400 in date. Some of the benches have old traceried ends. There are kneeling figures of Sir Edward Saunders and wife, d1573, and a tablet to two daughters of the Morgan family which is dated 1584.

WHATCOTE *St Peter* SP 298445

The nave north wall has two windows and a doorway with shafts which are Norman. The inner arch of the south doorway looks Norman too, but the outer arch is 13th century like the adjoining windows. The tower seems to be 13th century too, but with a 15th century top. The priest's door is of c1200. Otherwise the chancel is early 14th century but the east end was rebuilt after bombing damage in the Second World War. Three of the benches have old ends with blank tracery. The pulpit and communion rail are 18th century. There is a brass to William Auldynton, c1511. A later sundial lies upon the shaft of the medieval churchyard cross.

WHICHFORD *St Michael* SP 313346

The nave has some Norman masonry and a south doorway with one order of shafts, an arch with chevrons, and a tympanum with small motifs on the rim. The priest's doorway and piscina date the chancel to the 13th century although it was given windows with reticulated tracery in the 14th when the narrow south porch and the chapel east of it were added. The four bay north arcade is early 13th century. The aisle was widened c1300 after the tower at its west end had been begun, but older windows seem to have been reused. The chapel has some original glass and in a recess is a coffin lid with a cross and the Mohun arms of c1300. A tomb chest in the chancel has a brass of Rector Nicholas Asheton, d1582.

Whichford Church

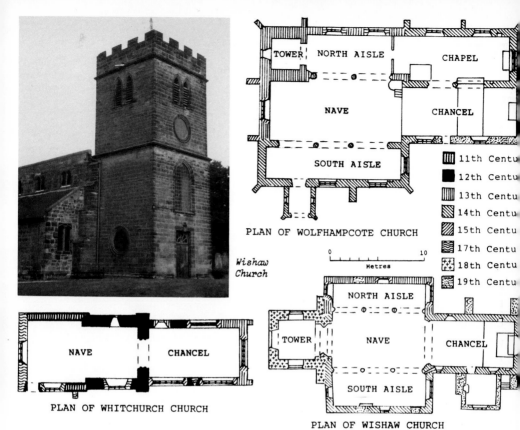

PLAN OF WOLFHAMPCOTE CHURCH

Wishaw Church

▦	11th Centu
■	12th Centu
▥	13th Centu
▧	14th Centu
▨	15th Centu
▩	17th Centu
▦	18th Centu
▦	19th Centu

0   10
Metres

PLAN OF WHITCHURCH CHURCH

PLAN OF WISHAW CHURCH

WHITCHURCH *St Mary*   SP 226486

The church lies alone in fields far from any road. The western part of
the nave with herringbone masonry is thought to be the east end of a
nave of c1100. The nave eastern part with thicker walls and corbel table
is Late Norman. With it go the chancel arch responds and parts of the
chancel. The nave has one window of c1300. The church was rebuilt in the
late 17th century when it was shortened and the present west wall built.
The 15th century windows in the chancel are said to have been inserted
then from elsewhere. The pulpit is Jacobean, and in the chancel is an
incised slab depicting Rector William Smyth, d1442.

WHITNASH *St Margaret*   SP 328637

Rebuilding in 1855, 1867, and 1880 has left only the 15th century tower
and brasses of Benedict Medley, d1503, and his wife, and Rector Richard
Bennet, d1532, in the chancel.

WIBTOFT *St Mary*   SP 480877

The west wall and a short section of the south wall are 13th century.
The rest is mostly rebuilt with old materials and a brick chancel added.

WILLEY *St Leonard*   SP 497848

The small oblong west tower and the nave north wall with several windows
and a polygonal rood loft stair turret are 15th century. The remainder
was rebuilt in 1864-5, when a porch and vestry were added. There is an
early 14th century effigy set into a slab with a cross of quatrefoils.

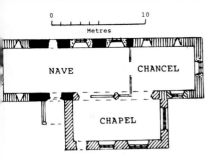

PLAN OF WIXFORD CHURCH

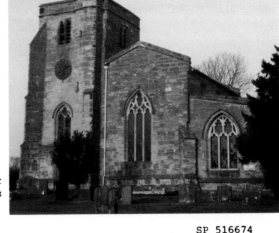

Withybrook Church

WILLOUGHBY *St Nicholas*   SP 516674

The earliest relic is the font with foliage, green men, and an animal. The fine tower is 14th century. The aisles with three bay arcades with piers of a complex section and the chancel arch are 15th century but the chancel itself is a 19th century brick structure. The north aisle may only be a remodelling of an older structure.

WISHAW *St Chad*   SP 177946

The west tower of c1700 still has gothic features. The north aisle with its three bay arcade is 13th century. The south aisle and chancel, with a squint between them, are early 14th century. The font is 18th century.

WITHYBROOK *All Saints*   SP 437841

The chancel doorway looks 13th century. The short NW tower and nave west wall are 14th century. The south aisle with a three bay arcade are late 14th century. The north aisle and chapel are about a century later. The chancel has an Easter Sepulchre with carvings of sleeping soldiers. One south arcade capital has fleurons. There are fragments of old glass in the south aisle windows. The communion rail is late 17th century. There is a brass of c1500 depicting a civilian, and an incised slab on a tomb chest depicts Sir Christopher Wright, d1602.

WIXFORD *St Milburgha*   SP 089549

The nave and chancel form a long single chamber. There are two Norman doorways, that on the south having columns, and several lancets of the time when the chancel was added and the west end rebuilt during the 13th century. The piscina and two south windows are 14th century. The south chapel of c1400 contains some old glass and a fine brass of Thomas de Cruwe and his wife, d1411, with a marginal inscription and canopies. The screen partly survives. There is a dug out chest on legs. A brass shows baby Rice Griffin, d1598. Lying loose is the head of a churchyard cross with a Crucifixion scene carved on it.

WOLFHAMPCOTE *St Peter*   SP 529653

The church lies alone in fields and is no longer used. The 14th century south aisle has a three bay arcade and windows with reticulated tracery. The late 13th century north aisle has only two bays, with 17th century windows, because a tower occupies what would be the third bay. The north chapel is late 14th century and the chancel is heavily restored. There are shafts rather than mullions on the 14th century screen. There are old benches and a late 17th century communion rail.

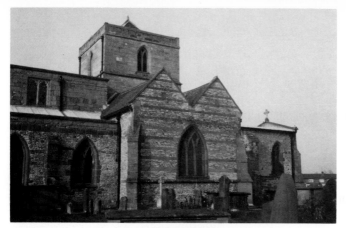

Wolston Church

Piscina, Wootton Wawen

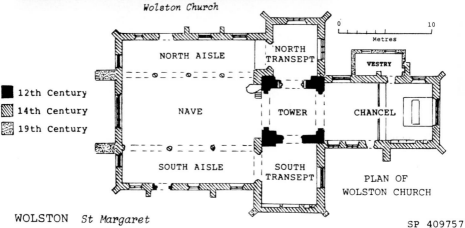

PLAN OF
WOLSTON CHURCH

12th Century
14th Century
19th Century

NORTH AISLE

NAVE

SOUTH AISLE

NORTH TRANSEPT

TOWER

SOUTH TRANSEPT

VESTRY

CHANCEL

WOLSTON St Margaret

SP 409757

The south doorway with one order of columns and the arches below the
central tower of 1760 are Norman. The three bay south arcade is earlier
than the four bay north arcade but both, like the aisle walls, chancel,
and the transepts of differing sizes are 14th century. The north transept
north window was altered in 1571 and 1624. The south transept has two
cinquecusped tomb recesses containing damaged effigies of c1300, and an
early 16th century monument of Purbeck marble which once bore brasses.
The chancel communion rails are of 1683 and have come from Rowington.
Another rail in the south transept is of similar date. The font probably
dates from the 17th century.

WOLVERTON St Mary

SP 206624

The 13th century nave has original doorways, a triple NW lancet, and a
pair of west lancets either side of a buttress. The chancel seems 14th
century although the east wall is rebuilt and the tomb recess is reset.
There are fragments of old glass on the north, and a 15th century font.

WOLVEY St John The Baptist

SP 431880

The Norman south doorway has two orders of columns and chevrons on the
arch. The south aisle is of c1300. The north aisle and the two effigies
of a knight and lady within it are of c1320-30, although the NE buttress
is dated 1630. Both arcades are of four bays. The chancel was rebuilt
in 1624, the year which appears over the east window, and again in 1858.
The font is partly 14th century, but with Victorian arcading.

70

Wootton Wawen Church

Harewell Brass

WOOTTON WAWEN *St Peter* SP 154633

This is one of the most interesting churches of
Warwickshire. It has work of every century from
the 11th to the 17th. Only the buttresses around
the varied exterior and the porch are later. The
story starts with the Late Saxon tower preserved
in the middle despite the way it restricts views
of the chancel from the nave. The arches to north
and south led to porticus or small side chapels.
Early in the 12th century the nave was rebuilt
much wider. In the 13th century a south transept
with a chapel east of it, and a south aisle with
a three bay arcade were added, and a large window
inserted in the nave north wall. The transept
and chapel were rebuilt along with the chancel
in the 14th century. Of the 15th century are the
tower top, clerestory, nave battlements, north
doorway and porch, the middle arch of the arcade,
the west window with busts of a king and queen
on the internal headstops, and the east window
with a leaf frieze. The aisle windows probably
date from the 1630s.

In the nave are bench ends with tracery and
poppy-heads, two parclose screens and a pulpit
which are all late medieval, and a 14th century
font. There is a 14th century chest on short legs.
The chancel has old glass in two windows and a
17th century communion rail. The chapel retains
its medieval barn-like roof and has murals. The
monuments include an alabaster effigy of a 15th
century knight, brasses of John Harewell, d1505,
and his wife on a tomb chest, an effigy of Francis
Smith, d1602, an urn to Robert Knight, d1744, and
a late 18th century triptych to Henry Knight.

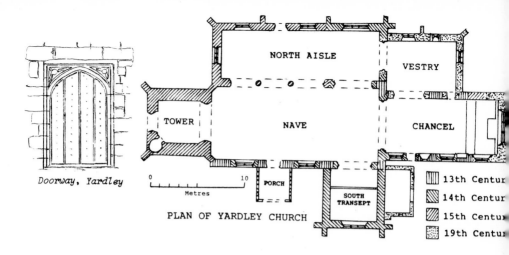

Doorway, Yardley

NORTH AISLE

VESTRY

TOWER

NAVE

CHANCEL

0   10

Metres

PORCH

SOUTH
TRANSEPT

PLAN OF YARDLEY CHURCH

13th Century

14th Century

15th Century

19th Century

WORMLEIGHTON *St Peter*   SP 447539

All four corners survive of the Norman nave. The three bay arcades and
the aisles and west tower are early 13th century. The aisles have early
and late 14th century windows. More occur in the chancel but this part
is much restored. The clerestory and the fine screen and loft are 15th
century and there are stalls with poppyheads, foliage, bishops, a dove,
an angel, and a hound. There are also old tiles. The communion rail and
altar panelling are Jacobean. There is a tablet to John Spenser, d1610.

WYKEN *Dedication Unknown*   SP 367807

Although within the boundary of Coventry this is still a mostly Norman
village church with fields to the east. There are several 12th century
windows in the nave and chancel and there is a contemporary font having
blank arcading. Several windows and the west tower are later medieval,
and part of a St Christopher mural remains on the north wall.

YARDLEY *St Eadburgha*   SP 135864

This is a large village church now within, but not dominated by, the
suburbs of Birmingham. The chancel and south doorway are 13th century.
Transepts were added in the 14th century and the chancel lengthened, and
in the 15th century the north aisle and west tower and spire were added.
In 1890 the south transept was partly rebuilt and the chancel extended
again and given a new NE vestry. In front of the south doorway is a 15th
century oak porch, and between it and the transept are 14th century
windows. The pulpit was given in 1627. By the tower is an incised slab,
once set on a tomb chest, bearing figures of Thomas Est, d1642, and his
wife. The south transept has a black marble tablet and bust of Edward
Est, d1703. In the chancel is a brass to Isabel Wheler, d1598, and a
peculiar monument to the Reverend Dr Henry Greswolde, d1700. It has a
curtained cave containing marble figures of him and his wife.

FURTHER READING

The Victoria County History of Warwickshire, several volumes.
Birmingham & West Midlands Archeological Society Transactions.
The Buildings of Warwickshire, Nikolaus Pevsner, 1974.